KU-322-577

Overcoming Common Problems Series

Overcoming Common Problems Series

Overcoming Common Problems

Stress at Work

Mary Hartley

First published in Great Britain in 2003 by
Sheldon Press
1 Marylebone Road
London NW1 4DU

© Mary Hartley 2003

All rights reserved. No part of this book may be reproduced
or transmitted in any form or by any means, electronic or
mechanical, including photocopying, recording, or by any
information storage and retrieval system, without permission
in writing from the publisher.

British Library Cataloguing-in-Publication Data
A catalogue record for this book is available from the British Library

ISBN 0–85969–858–0

1 3 5 7 9 10 8 6 4 2

Typeset by Deltatype Limited, Birkenhead, Merseyside
Printed in Great Britain by Biddles Ltd
www.biddles.co.uk

**SOUTH CHESHIRE COLLEGE
CENTRAL LRC**

Acc no......A004484......

Date..11.04.. Price...7.99... Supplier...CO...

Invoice No......523435...

Order No......40080......

Class no......616.98......

Contents

1
What is Stress?

The word 'stress' has become a part of our everyday vocabulary as a useful term to describe a range of experiences. We speak of feeling stressed when we are rushing to finish a task, or trying to do several things at once; we describe our jobs as stressful when we want to indicate how demanding our work is; we say we are stressed out when we get tired and irritable. What we are describing when we use the word is our reaction to pressure and challenge. Stress in itself is a positive force that spurs us into action in response to a demand, and a healthy amount of stress helps us to survive. However, stress becomes negative and harmful when we cannot cope with the demands that are made. When there is a gap between a situation and what we judge to be our ability to handle it, the resulting physical, emotional and mental strain is what we term 'stress'. Although stress itself is not an illness it can lead to ill health and life-damaging conditions.

The stress response

One of the reasons that human beings have survived so long is that we have a super-efficient system designed to help us to deal with threats. We have a response known as 'fight or flight', a term which refers to the automatic changes that are triggered in our bodies when we are faced with a life-or-death situation. What we need is a surge of strength to enable us to cope with the challenge, which in primitive times we would have done by fighting the enemy or running for our lives. This strength is supplied by the muscles and organs of the body, which suspend and divert their normal functions in order to support the action which is needed.

How it works

There are two branches of our central nervous system, the 'sympathetic' and the 'parasympathetic'. When the brain perceives a threat, the sympathetic side is activated and a series of changes takes place very rapidly.

Change	Reason for change
Heart rate increases	To pump blood rapidly to muscles and lungs to enable them to work more effectively
Breathing increases	To increase the amount of oxygen in the blood
Adrenaline and noradrenaline released	To stimulate reflexes and metabolism
Thyroid hormones released	To speed up metabolism
Liver releases sugar and fats	To boost energy
Digestion shuts down	To divert blood to lungs and muscles
Increase in sweating	To help you lose the heat that has been generated
Pupils of eyes enlarge	To enable you to see any source of danger

Once action has been taken, our bodies calm down and normal functions are resumed. The heart stops beating so quickly, the stress hormones are neutralized and the digestive system can function again. This is where the parasympathetic branch of our nervous system comes into play. This system is designed to make sure that our store of energy is built up and conserved. It creates a climate in which our bodies can rest and recover.

Why is there a problem?

The problem is that our bodies are programmed to respond to physical threats with rapid physical action. In today's workplace our challenges are not likely to be physical. We are put under pressure by the psychological, mental and emotional demands of dealing with workloads, interacting with a range of people, balancing conflicting needs, coping with difficult working conditions and the whole range of problems we face every day. We meet these pressures with an automatic response that was helpful in a previous era but is not appropriate now. The bodily changes which were designed as a short-term aid to survival become harmful if they are experienced too often and for too long. As the following examples illustrate, being in a heightened state over and over again with no corresponding release and return to normality can lead to stress-related illnesses.

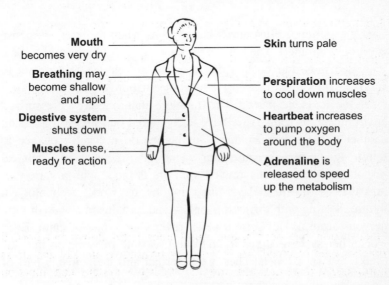

Mouth becomes very dry

Breathing may become shallow and rapid

Digestive system shuts down

Muscles tense, ready for action

Skin turns pale

Perspiration increases to cool down muscles

Heartbeat increases to pump oxygen around the body

Adrenaline is released to speed up the metabolism

Figure 1 Your body's reactions

Scene 1: One thing after another

Lara is late for her appointment. On the final stretch of motorway before her destination, traffic is reduced to a single lane of crawling vehicles. Seething with impatience, drumming her fingers on the steering wheel, she calculates to what extent this delay will throw out her remaining schedule. She tries to phone through to her next appointment but to her frustration she cannot get a signal on her cell phone.

The meeting is tricky. The client asks a number of questions to which Lara cannot give satisfactory replies because there has not been enough time for her to process the relevant figures – every

3

time she had started to do so, someone had interrupted her. As the meeting progresses she can feel her stomach churning and her heart beating rapidly. All her muscles are tense as she rushes to her following appointment

At the end of the day Lara has a headache and is tense and edgy. She finds it hard to get to sleep that night, as indeed is the case most nights.

Lara's experience illustrates what happens when the stress response is on constant alert. The body's response to stress enables us to deal with demands and challenges, and was developed to help us to survive. Our system gears up to meet the challenge, then calms down when the crisis has passed. The trouble is that in today's pressurized environment, as soon as we have encountered one stressful incident, another occurs, then another. Our bodies do not get a chance to return to normal because our natural hormonal and chemical responses are constantly revved up. Lara is faced with a variety of pressures – traffic delays, interruptions to work, technological failure, dealing with difficult people – and remains in a state of high nervous arousal. Her system never reverts to a state of calm. Even worse, her system begins to adapt to this state of being so that she thinks that severe headaches are a normal and unavoidable part of life.

Scene 2: An aggressive pupil

Sean can tell that Bradley is in an angry and restless mood. He has been needling other pupils before the lesson began, and has continued to issue threatening glances at those around him. When Sean asks the class to produce their homework for collection, Bradley says that he does not have the work. When Sean asks for the reason, Bradley gets to his feet and shouts at Sean that he is sick of being picked on.

Sean feels a surge of adrenaline rush through his body. His blood races to his limbs and his mouth goes dry. He is trembling and ready for action – but he cannot take the physical action for which his body has prepared him. His body is telling him to behave in a certain way, but he knows that he must override his body's messages. There is no outlet for this pent-up energy.

Sometimes Sean is in this situation several times during the course of a day. His health is being damaged by the constant chemical and hormonal assault on his nervous system. As the term goes on, Sean begins to suffer from stomach pains and finds it hard to concentrate.

Sean's experience demonstrates what can happen when the responses for which we are programmed cannot be followed through. When we encounter one of our stressors, our physiological system springs into action, giving us the energy either to fight what we perceive as the enemy, or to run for our life. Our bodies are teeming with biochemicals urging us to take rapid physical action, but the trouble is that we cannot physically attack a boss, colleague, customer or pupil, nor is running out of the office or workplace a viable option. The stress response remains, with no outlet, and the resulting build-up can lead to a range of illnesses.

The effects of stress in the workplace

The cost of illness

Sickness and absence

Stress itself is not an illness, but a range of illnesses and ailments are thought to be caused by stress, and there are many conditions that are made worse by stress. Some disorders are rooted directly in the stress response, in that there is a direct link between the physiological changes in our bodies that are designed to help us to deal with danger and the development of particular illnesses and diseases. Each change has a particular role in giving us a short-term surge of energy to cope with the emergency. Once the emergency has passed, our bodies are supposed to revert to their previous state. However, if we do not calm down, the changes can go on for a longer time than is healthy. If stress responses are too prolonged or frequent the bodily changes that they bring about can become harmful. Here are some examples:

Type of stress response activity	*Possible illness if it is prolonged*
Increased heart rate	Heart disease, hypertension, strokes, kidney damage, blood sugar disturbances, chest pain
Release of thyroid hormones	Exhaustion, weight loss, physical collapse
Release of cholesterol	Risk of hardening of arteries, leading to heart attacks and strokes
Tensed muscles	Aches, pains, postural and back problems, headaches, migraine
Close down of digestive system	Ulcers, stomach upsets, Irritable Bowel Syndrome

Other ailments which are recognized as having a stress background include allergies such as hay fever, rheumatoid arthritis and skin disorders such as eczema and acne. You may have noticed that when you are experiencing a stressful period you tend to pick up coughs and colds very easily, and seem to be a target for any bug or virus that is going round. One of the reasons for this is the constant presence of adrenaline and cortisone in the body, which weakens the immune system and lowers our resistance to infection and illness. The suppression of the immune system has also been linked with certain types of cancer.

Mental or emotional disturbances can also be the result of stress. Stress can cause depression and mental breakdown, and is often a factor in alcoholism and alcohol-related illnesses.

In economic terms, there is a price to pay for illnesses brought about by stress. The Health and Safety Executive calculates that about 500,000 workers in the UK experience illness caused by work-related stress, and that 6.5 million working days are lost each year.

Legal costs
Now that stress-induced illness is on an equal footing with other work-related illnesses or injuries, your company or organization may

become involved in expensive lawsuits. Organizations are now seen to be responsible for the physical and mental well-being of their staff, and it is a legal obligation to take reasonable care that employees are not put at risk through stress. Firms may find themselves facing claims of unfair dismissal or personal injury, or of having discriminated against someone with a disability. There is more about this in Chapter 7.

The cost of staff turnover

When people suffer unwelcome and harmful pressure at work, they often exercise the choice to leave and find another job. Finding a replacement can be a costly and lengthy process.

Mistakes and accidents

When we are under stress we are much more likely to make mistakes or to be careless. You might have noticed that during stressful periods you are far more 'accident-prone' than usual. You are tired, preoccupied, worried, distracted, overwhelmed, or experiencing any of a number of conditions which mean that your focus and concentration may be affected.

How stress affects your ability to work

Stress affects all areas of your human function. It affects the way that you behave, the way that you think and the way that you feel, as well as causing the physical ailments we have described. It is hardly surprising, then, that stress affects your capability to do your job.

Stress and your thinking processes

Scene 3: Tracey loses the plot

Tracey has recently started her own business designing and making wedding dresses. She is putting in hours and hours of work trying to build up her customer base and meet existing orders. Her client is describing the bridesmaid dresses that she wants.

'But perhaps a softer colour would be better. What do you think?'

7

'What? Oh, sorry, I . . .' Tracey is miles away. She just cannot concentrate on what the customer is saying. She pulls herself together and manages to cover up her lack of attention, but then later in the meeting she finds it hard to decide between the different design options that the client is considering. Feeling the need to make a decision, she chooses a design that is in fact not appropriate for the fabric.

After the meeting, Tracey is near to tears. She feels that she is not doing a good job and begins to wonder if she should have started this business. Creativity is essential to her work, and she feels that her ability to be innovative and come up with ideas is not as good as it used to be.

Tracey is showing symptoms of stress. When we suffer from too much pressure, our ability to think and to make decisions is impaired. We try to process information very quickly to keep up with demands, and cannot think effectively about complex issues. Our attention and our focus goes, and we can get things out of proportion.

Checklist: Stress and your mental abilities
Check any of the signs that you have noticed in yourself:

- poor decision-making;
- inability to concentrate;
- difficulty with thinking clearly;
- loss of creativity;
- memory getting worse;
- less able to plan your work;
- less able to prioritize;
- less in control of your work.

Your own examples:

_____

_____

Stress and your emotional state

Scene 4: Julian feels that he cannot cope

Julian deals face-to-face with customer enquiries and complaints. He is under pressure to deal with an increased quota of cases, and he has also experienced a number of unpleasant and abusive customers. Julian feels that he cannot cope with what is required of him, and often feels anxious and upset.

Stress unbalances our emotional equilibrium. It can bring about unwelcome changes in our feelings, causing us to experience emotional states which interfere with our sense of well-being and our ability to work effectively.

Checklist: Stress and your emotions
Check any of the signs that you have noticed in yourself:

- feeling upset and tearful;
- mood swings;
- feeling demotivated;
- feeling that you are a failure;
- feeling unable to cope;
- feeling powerless;
- being irritable;
- anxiety and apprehension;
- feeling panicky;
- feeling apathetic;
- withdrawing into yourself;
- lack of enjoyment;
- feeling angry.

Your own examples:

_____

_____

Stress and your behaviour

Scene 5: Ted's hyped-up behaviour

Ted is in overdrive. He tears around the building at top speed, and everyone notices that he speaks much more quickly than usual. He jumps and appears startled when someone speaks to him unexpectedly. Ted is busy all the time, but he puts his energy into low-priority or distracting tasks, and makes decisions too quickly.

After work, Ted tries to wind down with a fcw drinks. It seems to take an increasing amount of alcohol to help him to relax.

Our behaviour changes at the beginning of a period of stress arousal. Like Ted, we may experience a sense of urgency as stress rcsponse spurs us into heightened activity. As a result of the exhaustion which eventually sets in, we may show decreased activity, slumping into lethargy and lack of interest.

Checklist: How behaviour reveals stress
Check any of the signs that you have noticed in yourself:

- rapid movements;
- talking too loudly or too softly;
- craving for food;
- lack of appetite;
- increased use of prescription or other drugs;
- disturbance in sleep patterns;
- increased alcohol consumption;
- engaging in pointless activities;
- more accident-prone;
- unable to get going with tasks.

Your own examples:

Stress and your body

Scene 6: Lara's migraines

You may remember Lara from p. 3. She finds that her tension headaches develop into migraines which are hard to shake off. Her face and scalp muscles are constantly tight, and the overworked vessels supplying blood to her brain go into spasms. Her migraines are more and more easily triggered.

'She's got another migraine,' people at work say when Lara is off sick or is unable to work effectively. However, migraine is the symptom, not the disease. The 'disease', or what is really wrong with her, is stress.

Checklist: The physical signs of stress
Check any signs that you have noticed in yourself:

- back, shoulder, neck aches;
- heart palpitations;
- chest pain;
- headaches;
- stomach cramps;
- migraines;
- skin rashes;
- frequently picking up colds and other bugs that go around;
- bowel or urinary problems;
- fainting;
- breathlessness;
- loss of libido.

Your own examples:

_____

_____

The hidden costs of stress in the workplace

Stress-related illnesses are the biggest cause of absence from work and, as we have seen, the cost can be assessed in terms of sick leave, lost working days and impaired production. However, it is possible that Julian, Ted and Lara (and possibly you yourself) struggle on at work most of the time, feeling not quite on top of things, and trying to ignore or hide the symptoms of stress. Sooner or later, however, factors such as poor judgement and decision-making will take their toll. This may be measurable in terms of lost or decreased business, but what is less hard to measure is the cost to you and to the people with whom you work.

Personal cost of stress at work
Difficult relationships can cause stress at work, and people who are under stress can find it difficult to communicate and deal effectively with their co-workers, which leads to more stress ... and so the cycle continues. Personality clashes and unwelcome feelings and emotions damage healthy relationships, and everyone's work and personal well-being suffers. Goodwill is eroded, and motivation lessens.

Stress and the individual

We all respond to pressure in our own way. A number of factors, such as our individual genes, our emotional history, our life experiences, patterns of behaviour and patterns of thinking that we have inherited or developed, all affect the way we react. It is important to recognize and accept that your response may not be the same as someone else's. Your stressful event or situation may be someone else's stimulating challenge; you may experience head-aches as a result of too much pressure, whereas your colleague may have digestive problems. Learn to recognize your own signs of stress as soon as they appear. Look back at the symptoms that you marked in the checklists, and become aware of when and how your body and your mind start to tell you that the balance is tipping. There will probably be particular things that you start to do, and certain types of feeling that you begin to experience. You may notice these warning alerts yourself, or perhaps other people are more aware of them. For example, you might not realize that you are becoming very snappy and irritable, or that you have started to hum or whistle under your breath constantly, but those around you may very quickly pick this up as one of the signs that things are getting on top of you. Even your bodily response may be apparent to others, who might notice before you do that you are, say, dashing to the bathroom more frequently than usual. Raise your awareness of exactly how these signs of stress first show in your behaviour by monitoring them over a period of time. Get someone else to help you, perhaps someone from your support network (more about this in Chapter 5, pp. 102–5).

ACTIVITY 1: Stress alert

Emotional	*Warning sign*	*How I know*
Behavioural		
Physical		
Mental		

Managing stress in the twenty-first century

We have to learn to control our stress response and channel our energy into producing a response that is appropriate to the workplace in the twenty-first century. In demanding situations we are often required to use our judgement and to communicate clearly, behaviour which is difficult to produce when the body is churning with stress hormones urging us to take immediate action. Perhaps in years to come our bodies will adapt to the different circumstances, but in the meantime we can use approaches and strategies to prevent the harmful effects of stress, and to develop positive ways of managing pressure.

Our reaction to pressure is governed by our bodies and our minds, and the root causes of stress are physical and psychological. The close interaction of mind and body means that we can learn to manage our mental responses by psychological and physical means, and that we can learn to deal with physical tension by applying both mental and psychological approaches. There is a range of strategies to help you to short-circuit the stress response by activating the parasympathetic side of the nervous system and bringing about a feeling of relaxation and calm. Recognizing the signs and symptoms of stress and taking action to prevent harmful build-up is at the heart of successful stress management.

Your stress management plan

The following chapters will help you to develop your own plan for managing pressure.

The first step is to know yourself. **Self-knowledge** is essential. You have already begun to look at the signs of stress that you might exhibit. Back this up by identifying and exploring aspects of your character and personality and how they affect your response to pressure.

Once you have done this, you will be able to make a realistic assessment of what causes you to experience stress. When you can **identify your own stressors** you are in a position to make decisions about how you cope with them. You can **anticipate** what are likely to be stressful periods and put into place some strategies for coping.

The next step is to **choose how you deal with your stressors**. You have a number of options to consider: you can remove the stressor, alter your perception of the stressor, or change your behaviour. The important thing is that you are willing to go through the sometimes difficult and painful process of making changes. You might have noticed that we sometimes choose to endure a situation rather than face up to it and tackle it.

In order to prevent harmful stress in the future, you can try to **develop a resilient personality and lifestyle**. There are certain attitudes and habits of behaviour that will not only inoculate you against the worst aspects of stress, but will also help you to maintain a balanced and fulfilling working life.

2
Your Stress Profile

You and your job

A helpful way to start your assessment of your vulnerability to stress is by considering the job you are doing at the moment, and judging to what extent the job suits your character and personality.

Does the job fit?

If the work that you do satisfies none or few of your needs you are likely to experience the kind of boredom and frustration that can become stressful.

ACTIVITY 2: What I want from work

Read each of the following descriptions and mark each one A (essential to me), B (quite important, but doesn't matter that much), C (doesn't matter at all to me), D (I would hate this).

	A	B	C	D
1 Work that offers long-term employment prospects	☐	☐	☐	☐
2 Promotion prospects – a career ladder	☐	☐	☐	☐
3 Varied routine	☐	☐	☐	☐
4 Being clear about duties and objectives	☐	☐	☐	☐
5 Work that is challenging	☐	☐	☐	☐
6 Undemanding work	☐	☐	☐	☐
7 Lots of contact with people	☐	☐	☐	☐
8 Work that is involving	☐	☐	☐	☐
9 Work that completely absorbs me	☐	☐	☐	☐
10 Fringe benefits	☐	☐	☐	☐
11 Level of pay	☐	☐	☐	☐

12 Being in a position of power ☐ ☐ ☐ ☐
13 Being able to influence/make a difference ☐ ☐ ☐ ☐
14 Clear signs of status within the company ☐ ☐ ☐ ☐
15 Being able to get on with the job without being ☐ ☐ ☐ ☐
   hassled
16 Work that uses my specialist knowledge/skills ☐ ☐ ☐ ☐
17 Getting along with colleagues ☐ ☐ ☐ ☐
18 Socializing with colleagues outside work ☐ ☐ ☐ ☐
19 Having responsibility ☐ ☐ ☐ ☐
20 Opportunities for training/development ☐ ☐ ☐ ☐
21 Being able to express myself creatively ☐ ☐ ☐ ☐
22 Being respected by the public ☐ ☐ ☐ ☐
23 Lots of stimulation ☐ ☐ ☐ ☐
24 Feeling tranquil and outside the 'rat race' ☐ ☐ ☐ ☐
25 Work that is socially useful ☐ ☐ ☐ ☐
26 Being able to determine my own work agenda ☐ ☐ ☐ ☐

Your own ideas

27 _____ ☐ ☐ ☐ ☐
28 _____ ☐ ☐ ☐ ☐
29 _____ ☐ ☐ ☐ ☐
30 _____ ☐ ☐ ☐ ☐

Add up the number of times you have ticked each letter. An ideal job for you would be one which satisfies all your A requirements, a number of your B requirements and has none of your Ds.

However, even if your essential requirements are being met in the work that you are doing, you might still find aspects of your work stressful. For example, you might have fulfilled your need for responsibility and enjoy being in a responsible position at work, but find there may be aspects of the role, such as having to criticize people's performance, that you find stressful. Your work might give you sufficient challenge and absorption, but you might suffer the stressful effects of neglecting other areas of your life.

Your personal values

The above activity will also help you to determine your core life values. Your values are at the centre of the way you see the world and are what motivate you in your beliefs and behaviour. When you are clear about the nature of your personal values, or the things that matter most to you, you can assess to what extent they are supported and developed by the work that you do.

ACTIVITY 3: Identifying your personal values

Find the five values that matter most to you. There are some ideas below to get you going. Circle all the words which reflect what matters to you, and add your own ideas. Choose the five which matter most to you.

wealth	religion	travel	kindness
health	spirituality	achievement	learning
children	marriage	honesty	family
friends	financial security	freedom	excitement
social responsibility	humour	trust	compassion
creativity	intellectual growth	community	loyalty
open-mindedness	being a leader	discipline	self-sufficiency

Your own ideas:

_____

_____

My five most important values:

1 _____

2 _____

3 _____

4 _____

5 _____

_____

17

Personality and behaviour

Some people are more likely to suffer from high degrees of stress than others. Two people faced with the same pressure may react to it in very different ways, depending on a range of factors. One important factor is your personality type.

Type A (Attacking, Angry, Always in a rush)

Type A is a kind of personality particularly prone to stress which was identified in the 1970s by American cardiologists Drs Rosenman and Friedman. This group of people is prone to highly competitive and hostile behaviour, and has an increased risk of heart disease because their stress response is easily and frequently triggered, putting huge strain on the cardiovascular system.

Scene 7: A typical Type A

Owen speaks rapidly into his cell phone as he strides down the corridor to his office. 'We've got to beat them on this one,' he says. 'We need to come up with a better idea before they get back to the agency. I'll get the team on to it right away.' He fires off several emails on different matters before he takes off his coat, then goes to see Andrea. 'We need to do a new outline!' he barks. 'I knew that last one was rubbish.'

'We could have taken more time over it,' murmurs Andrea. Owen had pushed them to produce the outline in the shortest possible time because he had two or three other projects on the go at the same time. Now he moves restlessly as Andrea pulls up the details, drumming his fingers on the side of his chair.

'I'll just get a coffee and make a couple of calls while you do that,' he says. He walks towards the coffee machine as he speaks, and speeds up when he sees someone heading in the same direction. Owen gives a little smile of triumph as he gets there first.

Owen's behaviour demonstrates some typical Type A behaviour. He is highly competitive, to the extent that he sees even minor everyday occurrences in terms of winning. His behaviour is impatient and aggressive, and he is physically restless and hurried, doing several things at once and at a rapid rate.

ACTIVITY 4: Check your Type A characteristics

Are you constantly in a rush?
Do you find it hard to relax?
Do you do most things quickly?
Do you frequently challenge and confront others?
Do you switch off when others are talking?
Would people describe you as aggressive?
Do you do more than one thing at a time?
Do you try to pack more and more into less time?
Do little things make you angry?
Are you mentally super-alert?
Do people call you a workaholic?
Do you get a buzz from feeling stressed?

If you answered 'Yes' to a significant number of the questions in Activity 4, you could be lining yourself up for some very unpleasant physical and mental conditions as your system responds to the excessive demands being placed on it.

However, some Type A characteristics are those that are welcomed and rewarded in certain business environments. The drive and enthusiasm displayed by people in this group is highly valued, and their determination to achieve often results in high-status and highly paid positions. The dangerous aspects of this type of behaviour are not so much to do with hard work and achievement, but with the anger, frustration and resentment that accompany the restless striving and desire to win.

If you recognize aspects of this behaviour in yourself, you could try some strategies to manage your behaviour, and to direct your energy to developing optimum mental and physical fitness to enable you to achieve your utmost without harming your health.

Type B (Behaving calmly)

This type of personality is the opposite of Type A. Type B describes an unhurried, relaxed approach to work, which in fact can be just as effective – if not more so – as the restless, impatient behaviour of those at the other extreme.

Scene 8: Alan queues calmly

Alan is queuing for his season ticket, and can see that he will have to wait for some time. Accepting that he cannot change this situation, Alan passes the time by flicking through a newspaper. He keeps his body relaxed, and now and then glances at the queue and the activity around him, making the most of this opportunity to pause and do nothing.

Alan's behaviour shows characteristics typical of Type B. This personality is uncompetitive, not always in a hurry, and can take things one at a time. People in this category are able to relax, and are not plagued by feelings of guilt and anger. Their way of behaving is much healthier and far less stress-prone than Type A behaviour.

These two types represent extremes, and it is likely that your behaviour shows just some characteristics of a particular group. If you fall into the A category, it would be a good idea to adopt some aspects of Type B behaviour. Choose one or two specific activities that you can build into your daily routine – and reward yourself for each example of different behaviour.

Ways of managing Type A behaviour

Do things more slowly.

Do one thing at a time.

Use self-talk to reduce your time urgency: tell yourself, 'There's no hurry. Slow down.' You could make this a rhythmical incantation to help you to calm down.

Work on managing your feelings of hostility and anger.

Work on developing a balanced lifestyle.

Learn to say no.

Plan fewer activities for each day.

Leave more time than you think you need between activities.

Take breaks.

Get rid of unnecessary deadlines.

Your own ideas:

_____

_____

Type D (Distressed)

Another type of personality has been identified recently – Type D. D is for Distressed. The characteristics of this type are that they feel gloomy and pessimistic about life in general, worry a lot, often feel miserable and unhappy, but do not communicate these feelings. Instead, they bottle up their emotions at the expense of their physical and mental health. This is the crucial factor – you may feel generally negative and unhappy, but if you can express your emotions you are less likely to suffer the damaging consequences of keeping them bottled up.

Scene 9: Eileen bottles up her feelings

Eileen works as a legal secretary in a small firm. Her working conditions are good and she finds that the type and amount of work that she has to do gives her just the right amount of challenge. She has good friends, at work and outside, and a range of interests. Recently Eileen has experienced palpitations and chest pains which have become quite severe. Her friends and family are surprised to hear that Eileen's illness is stress-related – she always seems to be calm and in control.

What others don't know is that Eileen worries all the time. Although everything at work seems to be fine, she is in a constant state of tension and anxiety about the standard of her work and how she is perceived. If she makes a mistake, or is late with a piece of work, she worries that she will not keep her job. She imagines the very worst that might happen in this event, and this makes her worry more. Behind her calm and serene exterior, Eileen feels anxious, gloomy and unhappy. What contributes to her stress is that she keeps these feelings to herself.

21

ACTIVITY 5: Are you a Type D?

Fill in the chart to help you to see if your emotions and behaviour put you in this category. Think about unhappy feelings that you have experienced over the past month. Decide, if you can, what triggered them. Then record how you dealt with them.

	Feeling	Strength of feeling	Cause	What I did
(a)				
(b)				
(c)				

Ways of managing Type D behaviour

Acknowledge and accept your feelings.

Talk to a suitable friend about how you are feeling – let off steam.

Look for the root cause of your feelings – for example, are you angry with somebody? Are you frustrated by aspects of your working life?

Explore various ways of dealing with your unhappiness – for example, discussing an issue or situation with the person involved.

Develop assertiveness skills to help you to express your feelings appropriately.

Your own ideas:

Ways of thinking that can lead to stress

The way that we think about events and our individual perception of them affects our response. Every one of us perceives events in our own particular way, influenced by our personality, our needs and motives, our emotional history and the influences that have shaped us. We often see what we want to see, filtering out what does not interest or concern us and focusing on what meets our needs and matches or reinforces our view of the world. This process of filtering, which happens so quickly and unconsciously that we are not aware that it is happening, enables us to make sense of the huge amount of information that bombards our senses. For example, a group of people entering a workspace for the first time will take in different things. One person may notice health and safety aspects, such as fire precautions and the positioning of furniture and equipment, and not notice the colour of the walls, while someone else may respond immediately to the decor and atmosphere of a workspace, and another may focus on how up-to-date the technology is. These are natural, helpful responses. However, you may be seeing and interpreting events in a twisted or distorted way, discounting reality as you insist on forcing everything into your own skewed framework. It could be that when you are under pressure you put a negative slant on all events, or that you see things out of proportion. You may exaggerate situations, or be too hard on yourself or others. You may make false assumptions about events and people, or take everything too personally or emotionally.

The half-empty glass

The old cliché that an optimist sees a half-full glass and a pessimist sees a half-empty glass is relevant to stress management! The optimist knows that there is half a glass available to enjoy, and may believe that the glass may be refilled in some way, whereas the pessimist worries about there being only half a glass and about what will happen when that has gone. Those of us who constantly focus on the negative aspects of a situation are more likely to suffer under pressure than those who are able to see both the positive and negative sides. This does not mean that you should become unrealistically naive and blindly optimistic, but if your automatic response to events is negative, you may need to adjust your way of thinking. (We'll be looking at ways of doing this in Chapter 5.)

Scene 10: Ryan hears only the negative

'I thought you handled that interview very well,' Ryan's supervisor tells him. 'You were calm and patient, even when the client got angry. One thing concerns me – I don't think that the terms of the final agreement were entirely clear. Perhaps you should follow it up in writing.'

Ryan thinks, 'She's saying that I didn't do a good job. I should have made things clearer.'

Ryan automatically rejects the positive comments that were made. Even when he goes over what was said and realizes that he was praised by his supervisor, he rationalizes this by telling himself that the positive feedback doesn't count, or that it wasn't sincerely meant.

Out of proportion

Seeing things out of perspective can contribute to feelings of stress. We do this when we make things much worse than they really are, or go to the other extreme and discount or dismiss a genuine problem. Another way of getting things out of proportion is seeing them in absolute black-and-white terms. This leads to you making sweeping generalizations about how awful things are, possibly basing your assessment on a single event or comment. You may see yourself as a complete failure because of one mistake.

Scene 11: Ivan's mistake

Ivan has double-booked the speaker for a big conference. When he realizes his mistake he becomes very agitated, and is on the point of handing in his resignation. 'I'm hopeless at this job,' he says. 'I'll never be able to do it. I've made a mess of everything.' Ivan sees this setback as the first step in an inevitable catalogue of disasters as his career goes from bad to worse.

Personal blame

This is what you do when you blame yourself for everything that goes wrong. You take on the responsibility for the situation, even though you are not the cause. The other extreme of this kind of distorted thinking is blaming other people, and refusing to accept any personal responsibility.

Scene 12: Maggie's students fail their exam

Maggie made it clear to her students that they must complete their projects by the given deadline, and she gave them as much guidance and help as possible. Most of the group fulfil the requirements and receive satisfactory results. Two students do not hand in their work on time, and do not receive a grade. Maggie blames herself for their failure. She keeps telling herself that she should have done more to help them, and that it is entirely her fault that the two students did not complete their work in the allocated time.

Assuming the worst

We create stress for ourselves by jumping to conclusions about situations and people's behaviour, usually in an emotional response that disregards what may be the real facts.

Scene 13: He's getting back at me

Arlene sees that she has been put down for the late shift again. 'He's doing that on purpose,' she thinks. 'He's getting back at me because I had some time off last month.'

Arlene assumes that there is a deliberate intention to make things difficult for her, and that she is being made to pay for something that she has done.

Being too hard on yourself

Another common source of stress is a kind of irrational thinking that requires ourselves and others to behave according to unrealistic standards. You might have fixed ideas about the way that the world should be, and the way that people should behave. You might set yourself very rigid standards, and become very stressed and angry with yourself when you feel that you let yourself down by failing to behave according to the ideals you have established.

Scene 14: Khan wants to be perfect

Khan believes that a manager should never be seen to make a mistake. He thinks that he should do everything perfectly, as an example to his team. Khan's belief is that if he is seen to fall below the exacting standards that he sets, his credibility will suffer, and he will not be able to demand a high standard of work from his team.

We put ourselves under enormous pressure by hanging on to ideas about what 'should' happen and what we 'must' or 'ought to' do or be. Often we place an obligation on ourselves by using the word 'should' when in fact there is no legal or moral necessity to behave in a certain way. It is just an idea that we have, possibly one that has been inherited from our childhood authority figures and is no longer helpful or relevant – if it ever was.

How to straighten out distorted thinking

You can put right the kind of thinking error described above and break unhelpful patterns of thought that are contributing to stress. It does take time and commitment to stop established ways of thinking and to develop new approaches, but you will find that your stress levels decrease as you change your negative perceptions into more helpful appraisals of situations.

Challenge your thoughts

When you feel yourself getting into a stressful state, stop and identify the thoughts that are running through your mind. Find a statement to replace the negative or irrational thought with a more realistic and positive response. You could go through this process at the end of every day.

Situation: Being appraised by my supervisor.
What I thought: I've done everything wrong.
Distortion: Seeing only the negative.
Less stressful thought: I've done some things well.

Situation: Forgetting to pass on a message.
What I thought: This is absolutely terrible. She will never forgive me.
Distortion: Getting it out of perspective.
Less stressful thought: It's not that bad. It was just a mistake. It won't matter for very long.

Situation: Losing a client.

What I thought: It's all Bill's fault. He didn't handle them properly.

Distortion: Looking for someone to blame.

Less stressful thought: No one is entirely to blame. There are lots of factors involved. We could analyse how this situation arose and look at ways of preventing it from happening again.

Situation: I had a serious disagreement with a colleague, then saw her speaking privately to my boss.

What I thought: She's obviously complaining about me.

Distortion: Jumping to conclusions.

Less stressful thought: She may not be complaining. I could find out what was going on rather than make assumptions.

Reassess your beliefs about your own behaviour

A major source of stress is trying to live up to ideals that you set yourself. Of course, it is a good thing to set and maintain high standards for yourself. The problem arises when your personal standards and ideals are unrealistic or inappropriate, and are applied automatically without any analysis of what the particular situation requires. This is what happens with Khan in the previous scene. As he sees it, every demand requires a response that is 100 per cent perfect. You impose unnecessary pressure on yourself to behave in a way that complies with your personal contract with yourself, especially if your standards are based on ideas that are arbitrary and do not help you to behave effectively in every situation.

You can reduce your personal pressure by getting rid of the stranglehold of limiting beliefs and ideas. Changing the words you use can help to change the way you look at and feel about situations. Instead of expressions such as 'must', 'ought' or 'should', use other, less prescriptive words such as 'may' or 'could', 'would like to', 'want to' or 'will'. These words remind you that you have a choice, and they tap into your personal motivation, thereby reducing self-pressure.

Old thought	*New thought*
I must get this presentation absolutely right.	I really want to get it 100 per cent right, but if I don't, I can live with it.
I should never appear to be uncertain.	I may show uncertainty if I wish. It isn't a crime.
I must get this report finished today.	I will/would like/intend to get this report finished today.
I should put the needs of the team first.	I can put my own needs first sometimes.
I should accept things that I disagree with.	I have a right to say no or express disagreement.

Get into the habit of rethinking or challenging the ideas that govern your behaviour in particular situations. Khan, for example, could choose one or two instances in which he knows there is no need for 100 per cent perfection.

ACTIVITY 6: New beliefs for old

Identify situations at work in which your ideas about how you should feel or behave cause you extra pressure. For each example, decide what belief lies behind it – you may find that just one or two ideas influence you in a number of situations – and work out a new statement for yourself.

Situation: _____

Underlying belief: _____

New thought: _____

Situation: _____

Underlying belief: _____

New thought: _____

Situation: _____

Underlying belief: _____

New thought: _____

Situation: _____

Underlying belief: _____

New thought: _____

Reassess your beliefs about other people's behaviour

You might also have unhelpful beliefs about how others should behave at work. You may feel frustrated and annoyed when people's behaviour goes against your ideas and principles, and you might find that you are constantly coming into conflict with your co-workers because they are not living up to your own standards. In every workplace, certain standards are expected. There are requirements, some written, some unwritten, about how people should work and behave. It is reasonable to assume that people will generally try to meet these requirements. However, if in addition to these you have your own, internal, personal set of requirements, it is unreasonable to expect others to keep to them.

Scene 15: Kylie's appearance

Kylie is a junior technician in a laboratory, where Helen supervises her. Kylie has a stud in her nose and two rings in her eyebrow, and wears T-shirts with slogans on the front. Although the company dress code is casual and many of the younger staff dress in a similar way, Helen feels strongly that this is inappropriate for the workplace. 'I've always dressed conventionally for work,' she complains. 'I think that's the right thing to do. It shows that you take your work seriously.'

Helen gets very worked up about the situation, and feels tense every morning as she waits to see what Kylie is wearing today. She finds that she cannot supervise Kylie's work in a positive way. Helen's stress is caused by her belief that people should dress for work in the way that she thinks is appropriate.

You can reduce self-pressure by updating your beliefs about other people. Again, changing the words that you use will help you to change the way that you think. Instead of saying that people 'should' or 'ought to' behave in certain ways, find expressions that acknowledge the rights of others to their own choices. You could try prefacing your new statements with a phrase such as 'I would prefer' or 'People have a right'.

Old thought	New thought
People should be honest.	I would prefer people to be honest.
People ought not to waste the firm's time.	Others may choose to waste the firm's time. I choose not to behave in this way.
People should keep strong feelings to themselves in the workplace.	People have a right to express their feelings.

Practise rethinking your attitude. Helen, for example, could think, 'I don't like the way that Kylie dresses. However, her appearance is her choice. I do not have to like it, but I can choose to accept it.' Helen could go further and tell herself, 'My ideas were formed some time ago, and the world of work has changed. I could adjust to a different way of seeing things.'

ACTIVITY 7: Acknowledging others' rights

Identify situations at work in which your ideas about how others should feel or behave cause you extra pressure. For each example, decide what belief lies behind it – you may find that just one or two ideas influence you in a number of situations – and work out a new statement for yourself.

Situation: _____

Underlying belief: _____

New thought: _____

Situation: _____

Underlying belief: _____

New thought: _____

Situation: _____

Underlying belief: _____

New thought: _____

Situation: _____

Underlying belief: _____

New thought: _____

Talk yourself down

You can manage your thought processes to bring yourself into a less anxious state. When you are facing a difficult situation, use calm and rational self-talk before, during and after the event.

Scene 16: Martha takes charge

Martha is about to have her first shift in charge of the medical ward. She begins to worry about all the things that might go wrong, and doesn't feel confident of her ability to cope. Then she calms herself down with statements such as, 'I'm fully trained for this. I will be fine. I know what I am doing. I will cope with emergencies.'

As the day continues, Martha deals with surges of anxiety by reminding herself, 'Everything is going well. I can overcome difficulties.' She feels tense as she observes that one of the junior nursing staff is getting a bit flustered about changing a dressing, but thinks, 'I'll keep an eye on her, and make sure that she has help if she needs it.' In this way Martha channels her stress into a constructive plan, reducing her own anxiety and helping her to keep calm.

When her shift is over, Martha says to herself, 'That went well. I handled most things competently. Next time will be a lot easier.'

Another way of applying this strategy is to bring yourself into a less stressful state by asking yourself staged questions about the situation. Martha could prepare for her first day by asking herself:

What is the very worst that could happen today?
How likely is that to happen?
If it does happen, what could I do?
Are my anxieties about today caused by distorted thinking?
What will today seem like when I look back on it in a month's time? In a year's time?

This kind of calming self-talk is particularly effective when combined with breathing and relaxation exercises.

Use coping imagery

Another way of managing the anxiety you feel when you anticipate a stressful event is to imagine yourself in the dreaded situation. See yourself doing whatever it is, giving the presentation, attending the interview, dealing with the difficult customer. First of all, run through the event in your head, and jot down the parts that worry you the most. You might worry about not being able to answer questions, or that you will lose your temper with somebody, or that you will drop your notes all over the floor. Whatever it is, decide what you will do if that should happen.

Project yourself into the future and imagine yourself at each stage of the encounter. See yourself in the situation, coping with the difficulties that may occur.

Use the following chapters to help you to expand your self-knowledge and awareness of what causes you stress at work, and to identify a range of short- and long-term strategies for making any changes that will help you to cope with pressure.

3

Causes of Stress at Work

Although we all have our own personal response to events, certain factors have been identified as common causes of stress in the workplace.

Long hours

In spite of legislation intended to rationalize the length of working hours, employees in the United Kingdom are actually increasing the amount of time they spend at work or dealing with work matters at home. Although the Working Time Directive introduced in 1998 set a limit of an average of 48 hours that people could be required to work each week, many employees opt out of this because of the demands of the job and the expectations of their workplace. Unsociable hours, having to take work home and having too many demands on the time available all contribute to stress and tension. If you regularly work more than 40 hours a week you are unlikely to be operating at peak effectiveness and efficiency, and you are heading for damaged health and a shortened working life. Not only this, but the time that you put in is counterproductive and could result in you making mistakes and exercising poor judgement in the way that you deal with people and with work tasks.

Scene 17: Barry's long week

Barry's working day gets longer and longer. He stays on when most other people have left, and usually arrives home in the middle of the evening. He leaves very early in the morning to get a good start. At weekends he sometimes has to lock himself away to get on with a project, and he frequently sends work-related e-mail messages. Barry says that this is the only way he can get through the work.

'Do you really have to work like this?' Jenny asks him. She is close to tears, and Barry can hear the desperation in her voice.

When she's calmed down a bit she tells Barry that he's not looking well and she's getting tired of hardly ever seeing him. She ends by saying, 'Beth and Harry are starting to forget what their dad looks like!'

ACTIVITY 8: The hours you work

	Sometimes	Often	Frequently
Do you feel that you have too much work to do?	☐	☐	☐
Do you take work home?	☐	☐	☐
Do you cancel social or family engagements because of work?	☐	☐	☐
Do you work long hours?	☐	☐	☐
Do you work unsociable hours?	☐	☐	☐

How you could reduce stress in this area:

Learn some time management techniques.
Be clear about your personal goals.
Use positive self-talk to help you to keep to realistic hours.
Examine your work/life balance and make the desirable adjustments.
Learn to say no to requests.
Learn to ask for more time.

Your working environment

Your feelings at work and the effectiveness of your performance are influenced by your surroundings. We respond differently to different environments. Some of us like a buzzy atmosphere with lots of noise and activity, others prefer to work in calm, quiet surroundings. Even surroundings which seem welcoming and pleasant can impose strain and have an adverse effect on physical and mental health.

Space and privacy

You might find working in an open-plan space distracting and uncomfortable. Some of us, particularly those with very strong territorial instincts, find the lack of privacy a cause of tension. Compartmentalized workspaces provide a feeling of control and security, but may contribute to work stress by making communication difficult.

Working on a screen

You might find that you suffer from physical ailments such as eyestrain, back problems, muscular problems, headaches and repetitive strain injury, and that your mental well-being suffers as well as you become tired and irritable and lose concentration.

Wrong kind of light

Natural light is important to our well-being. It regulates our supply of melatonin, which in situations lacking natural light may build up to levels which could cause you to feel tired and depressed. Working in light that is too bright or too dim may cause headaches and eyestrain. Light that is unnaturally bright can lead to a feeling of disorientation – fluorescent lighting is particularly difficult to live with.

Comfort and decor

The colours and style of furniture and decoration can affect your mood. Bright colours can be stimulating, and drab or dreary colours might get you down. The kind of chair you use can affect the way you feel – it should be the right height for you, support your back, and should be placed at the right distance from your workstation. Furniture that is badly designed and positioned causes aches and pains, and the physical strain you experience can affect your mood and feelings.

Air quality

Air conditioning systems can cause a range of complaints such as sore eyes and allergies, while central heating dries out the atmosphere. If you work in air that is too dry you may suffer from respiratory problems and throat disorders. The Health and Safety Executive suggests that the working temperature should be between 16°C (60°F) and 24°C (75°F). If your job involves little exercise, the best temperature is towards the higher end of the scale.

Noise

Many workplaces have a high level of background noise – machinery, phones, voices and so on. Because we adapt to our surroundings you may not even be aware that you are constantly in the presence of noise, but its cumulative effect can cause you to feel edgy and bad-tempered, and can affect your ability to concentrate.

ACTIVITY 9: Your working environment

Think about the conditions in which you work. Identify three aspects which have a positive effect on you, and three aspects which have a negative effect.

	Positive	Negative
1		
2		
3		

How you could reduce stressful working conditions:

Follow safety guidelines.

Take regular breaks from looking at your VDU – do some stretching and relaxing exercises, and glance away from the screen at frequent intervals.

Lower the noise level where you can – turn down the volume on your phone, for example.

Keep noisy or constantly humming machines away from work areas.

Personalize your workspace with items such as plants, cards, pictures.

Introduce colours that help you to create and maintain an appropriate mood.

Speak to your manager or supervisor about any concerns or suggestions.

Develop communication and assertion skills to help you to deal confidently with these matters.

Conflict at work

Role ambiguity

A common source of stress is not being clear about the nature and scope of your work role. When your instructions or brief are unclear or lack sufficient detail you may experience intense anxiety as you proceed without really knowing what you should be doing: for example, whether you are exercising too much responsibility or too little in the execution of a task. If you are not sure of the relative importance of different aspects of your job you will find it impossible to prioritize your tasks and to decide how much time to allocate to different areas, which is a stressful situation to be in.

Scene 18: Kathy is uncertain about her role

Kathy has been given responsibility for setting up a meeting for the public. This involves tasks such as getting the venue prepared, arranging for adequate seating and refreshments, sorting out the details of the Powerpoint presentation and so on. On the day of the event she notices that the floor hasn't been properly cleaned, and approaches the department in charge of this area of work. To her surprise she gets quite a frosty reception, with the person to whom she speaks saying that it is not Kathy's place to comment on their work.

Kathy feels powerless in this situation. She knows she has to deal with the matter, or take the blame for the dirty appearance of the room. Either way puts her in a difficult situation. She has been given responsibility for a project, but the scope of her authority has not been made clear.

Role conflict

We experience role conflict when a particular aspect of our job contradicts another aspect. When different requirements appear to be incompatible we seem to be in a no-win situation in which satisfying one area will mean ignoring another, or will create difficulties in fulfilling that part of the job. You might find that there is a clash between your concern for individuals and the legal or procedural requirement of your job, or between your loyalty to your company and your obligation to clients or customers.

Scene 19: Jenny's role conflict

Jenny is a teacher with pastoral responsibility for a year group. In her pastoral role she has to attend and contribute to case conferences with Social Services about the welfare of individual pupils. At the same time, she has to meet and deal with these pupils in lessons. Jenny finds it very difficult to reconcile these two aspects of her role.

ACTIVITY 10: Your role at work

To what extent do the following statements apply to you?

	Agree	Partly agree	Disagree
1 I have too many roles	□	□	□
2 I am not sure what is expected of me	□	□	□
3 I am not sure how well or badly I am doing	□	□	□
4 There are frequent changes in what is expected of me	□	□	□
5 My goals and objectives are not clear and consistent	□	□	□
6 I am not clear what my priorities are	□	□	□
7 I often face conflicting demands	□	□	□

Conflict of values

Another source of conflict could be a clash between your personal value system and what is required of you at work.

Scene 20: Liz experiences a conflict of values

Liz enjoys her job as a researcher in a scientific institution. She can use her specialist knowledge and her analytical skill. She likes her colleagues and the working environment, and hopes to be promoted to team leader. When the organization secures a contract with a company which is developing genetically modified products Liz is given responsibility for this area of research.

At first Liz meets the new challenge very effectively. However, she begins to have stomach aches and digestive problems, which she attributes to her anxiety to succeed in her new position. At a social gathering one evening when she is asked what she is working on, Liz becomes highly defensive and gives a heated and confused account of the nature of her work. This makes her realize that she is very uncomfortable with the subject matter of her research, to such an extent that the mismatch between her values and her job is making her ill.

ACTIVITY 11: Does your work reflect your values?

In Chapter 2 you identified your main work and life values. How do they fit into the work that you do?

Value	How my work reflects this value	How my work contradicts this value
1		
2		
3		

4 _____

5 _____

How you could reduce stress in areas of role conflict:
  Discuss your role with your manager.
  Ask for any changes that you would like.
  Develop assertion skills to help you to do this confidently.
  Learn to say no to certain demands.
  Set clear goals and objectives.

Conflict between home and work

Whereas a supportive family and home environment can be a safe place and a refuge, enabling us to unwind and keep a sense of perspective about work, the conflicting demands of work and our personal lives can be a source of stress. Responsibility for children and dependants clashes with work responsibilities, the demands of work lead to a neglected or damaged social life, personal relationships suffer and feelings of guilt and resentment grow. The pressures of managing two careers can lead to stress and conflict.

Working from home can cause problems. Even with a dedicated space for working, it can be difficult to prevent work matters from spilling over into home life. If you are in this situation, you could establish boundaries in order to protect your personal life.

How you could reduce home/work conflict
  Examine your goals and priorities.
  Do not take work home with you.
  Do not take work-related calls at home.
  Establish a balance between work and home.
  Set a limit on the length of time in which you can complain about
    work.
  Change into different clothes when you come home from work or
    when you finish your day's work at home.

Relationships at work

You and your manager

Many people find that their relationship with their manager is a source of stress. You might feel that you are put under a lot of pressure, or feel that you do not have much support or encouragement. It can be stressful to feel that your manager is distant and uninterested in you, or that all the feedback you get is negative. This can make you feel undervalued and can affect your attitude to work, causing you to lose enthusiasm and motivation.

Relationships with co-workers

Dealing with other people can be stressful. Personality clashes, differences of opinion, conflicting goals and misunderstandings are just some of the ways in which our relationships with colleagues cause pain and pressure. It can be stressful to be with people who moan constantly, or whose humour we find unacceptable, or who use put-downs all the time. You may work with people who keep interrupting you, or who jump to conclusions and make assumptions about your behaviour.

Other situations that raise stress levels include:

- saying yes when you want to say no;
- knowing that you should reprimand or deal firmly with someone, but not wanting to;
- having strong feelings that you do not express appropriately.

Add your own ideas:

_____

_____

_____

_____

_____

ACTIVITY 12: What behaviour do you find difficult?

Ring any phrases that apply to you. Choose the three that are the most stressful for you. Identify the particular situations.

being criticized	expressing positive	saying no
dealing with put-downs	feelings	giving praise
accepting praise	expressing negative	asking for what I
giving criticism	feelings	want or need

Behaviour	*Example*

1 _____

2 _____

3 _____

How you could reduce stress in your relationships at work:

Communicate clearly.

Listen actively.

Learn to ask questions constructively.

Learn to be assertive in asking for what you want.

Learn to say no.

Express your feelings appropriately.

Give and receive praise and positive feedback confidently.

Give and receive criticism and negative feedback confidently.

The job itself

Level of activity and stimulation

When the pressure level at work is wrong for you, you are likely to experience symptoms of stress. Too much or too little pressure can be equally harmful.

ACTIVITY 13: What level of pressure are you experiencing?

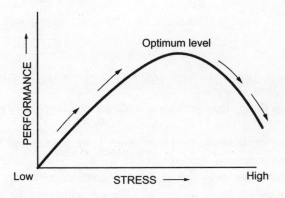

Figure 2 The pressure curve

What level of pressure are you experiencing at the moment? Mark it on the curve in Figure 2.

The skills needed for the job

Being unsure of your capability to do a job can be a source of stress. You might be uncomfortable with your levels of responsibility or your lack of competence in certain areas of your job. Maybe you are nervous about using technology. Your job might involve addressing large groups of people, which fills you with dread, or speaking at meetings, which makes you feel very anxious.

Training and development

Lack of clear opportunities to grow and develop can be a source of dissatisfaction, as can a lack of promotional opportunities.

Not being clear about what is expected

Lack of clarity about our work objectives can lead to stress. Being unsure about what we should be doing or if we are doing the right thing imposes great strain. If you do not receive effective feedback about your performance you can feel demotivated and isolated.

A plan for managing stressful aspects of the job itself

The following three steps provide a path for tackling these issues:

1 *Acquire self-knowledge.* Be clear about your values and goals, your strengths and weaknesses.
2 *Communicate.* Develop the skills and confidence to approach appropriate people about aspects of your job which are the source of pressure.
3 *Take responsibility for your development.* Show that you have the ability and the personal skills to build on your strengths and to improve your knowledge and abilities.

The culture of the organization

If the company you work for does not suit your personality and is not one in which you can achieve your personal and professional goals, you may well experience severe stressful dissatisfaction. When the culture, norms and expectations of your workplace are at odds with your own attitudes and outlook, you may feel out of place and that you are not valued.

ACTIVITY 14: How well do you match?

This exercise will help you to identify some aspects of the organizational culture of your place of work. For each item, think of a brief description, then mark on the scale the extent to which you are comfortable with this aspect of the organization.

Factor	Comfortable								Uncomfortable
Size	1	2	3	4	5	6	7	8	9
Public image	1	2	3	4	5	6	7	8	9
Organizational structure	1	2	3	4	5	6	7	8	9
The values of the organization	1	2	3	4	5	6	7	8	9
The kind of people who succeed or are powerful in the organization	1	2	3	4	5	6	7	8	9
How work is praised/criticized	1	2	3	4	5	6	7	8	9
How employees are shown to be valued/important	1	2	3	4	5	6	7	8	9
The way decisions are taken	1	2	3	4	5	6	7	8	9
Attitude to clients or customers	1	2	3	4	5	6	7	8	9
The way people speak/behave to each other	1	2	3	4	5	6	7	8	9
The way people dress	1	2	3	4	5	6	7	8	9
The company jargon	1	2	3	4	5	6	7	8	9

Your own ideas:

_____	1	2	3	4	5	6	7	8	9
_____	1	2	3	4	5	6	7	8	9
_____	1	2	3	4	5	6	7	8	9
_____	1	2	3	4	5	6	7	8	9

ACTIVITY 15: Your main work stressors

Decide which aspects of work are the most stressful for you. Be as precise as you can. Describe your feelings and behaviour in each situation.

	Stressful situation	*How I feel*	*How I behave*
1			
2			
3			
4			
5			
6			

4

Dealing with Stress at Work

How you cope at the moment

Now that you are aware of your own symptoms and sources of stress,
take some time to think about the strategies you use to deal with them.
It is possible that some of the habits that you have developed are in fact
not helpful. There are some attitudes and behaviours that may enable
you to get through the day-to-day business of work, and are effective in
the short term, but unless you deal with the central situation,
acknowledging your stress and finding positive ways of coping with it,
then you are just papering over the cracks.

Unhelpful habits

Denying what's happening

Sometimes it seems easier to pretend that nothing is wrong than to
face the situation. We try to convince ourselves and others that there
are rational explanations for our behaviour. We say that we are
working very long hours because there is particular pressure on at
the moment, and the situation will improve once this period is over.

Blaming others

This is a way of avoiding taking responsibility for ourselves. We
remove ourselves from the situation, wiping out our own contribution
to what is happening. Convinced that something or someone else is to
blame, we feel that it is not up to us to deal with the situation. If we
have a fraught relationship with someone, we describe the other person
as being difficult or impossible to work with.

Running away

You may deal with the situation by escaping from it. Rather than
deal with the issues that you have with a supervisor, you find another
job. Rather than speak to a difficult client or customer, you arrange
to be unavailable whenever they call. We can also 'run away'

emotionally, by withdrawing from a situation and refusing to be involved. In the short term this strategy works, but it does not get to the root of the problem, and by behaving in this way you are not giving yourself a chance to develop positive strategies for coping.

Repressing feelings

Keeping your feelings bottled up and buried won't get rid of them. In the short term you can bury your thoughts and emotions, and find a way of justifying this by telling yourself that it's better not to create unpleasantness, and that you will make matters worse by saying things that are better left unsaid. However, your feelings don't go away, and even if you get through the immediate situation in this way, what you have buried will emerge in some form when you meet the same or a similar situation again.

Living in the past

One way of dealing with change or challenge is dwelling on the time that has passed, when things were different. This way of dealing with an uncomfortable situation doesn't help you to deal with current stress. You might fall into kinds of behaviour and attitudes that you showed in the past, perhaps as a child, such as looking to other people for protection, or sulking. You constantly tell yourself that things were better before, and that there is nothing you can do about the present situation.

ACTIVITY 16: What are your unhelpful coping strategies?

These strategies are examples of how our way of dealing with a stressful situation is to avoid dealing with it directly. Identify any of these strategies which you use. An example has been done for you.

Situation	How I deal with it	Type of strategy
Having to cover up for a colleague's mistakes	Keep on doing it and hope he will leave	Running away

	Situation	How I deal with it	Type of strategy
1			
2			
3			

Positive strategies

You will deal more effectively with stressful situations at work if you face up to them and make rational decisions about the best way they could be handled. Once you have identified your own sources of stress, as you did at the end of the last chapter, you can look at the options that are open to you.

Decide what cannot be changed

Stand back from the situation and think about what aspects of it cannot be altered. For example, you probably have little choice about the people with whom you work – your 'difficult' manager is likely to remain your manager, or on leaving may be replaced by someone you consider to be similar or worse. You might be unable to change your contractual obligations, or certain conditions in your workplace. You cannot change other people's characters and personalities, or make them behave as you would like them to.

ACTIVITY 17: What cannot be changed?

What stressful aspects of your work cannot be changed?

	Example	Why it is fixed
1		
2		

3 _____

_____

Decide what can be changed

You may be able to change rather more than you think. There could be some aspects of troublesome relationships or some aspects of your job that could be altered. For example, you might be stuck with a difficult boss or team member, but you could think about improving your relationship with him or her. You may see your journey to work as an inescapable source of stress, but you could think of ways in which it could become less stressful.

It is helpful to think about what outcome you want, and then consider ways of achieving it.

_____

ACTIVITY 18: Deciding on the outcome

Choose three stressful work situations that you would like to change. In each case, describe the new situation you would like to bring about. An example has been done for you.

Situation	What I would like
Feeling overwhelmed by too much work	To manage my workload so that I feel more in control

1 _____

2 _____

3 _____

_____

Decide how to change

How are you going to bring about the desired change and so reduce your stress levels? There are several possibilities, some of which require you to develop a range of personal and practical resources.

Remove the stressor

You might be able to remove or reduce the source of stress. This could be the first option that you consider. For example, if you identify travelling to work as a major cause of stress, you could eliminate that factor by moving closer to work, or finding another job. Sometimes taking a major step to reduce a source of pressure is possible and indeed the best solution. It is more likely, however, that such a drastic step is neither feasible nor desirable, and you may prefer to employ other strategies.

Make a list of your practical options. Consider pros and cons. If you're under too much pressure to think clearly, ask a friend to help you to think things through.

Change your attitude

You could look at the situation in a different way. Check for the kind of negative and distorted thinking that we discussed in Chapter 2, and develop a new attitude to your stressor. If you are applying negative judgements and irrational thoughts, work out for yourself a different appraisal of the situation. Write it down and practise saying it. Behave in a way that supports it.

Scene 21: Liz works through her options

You may remember Liz from the previous chapter, who is experiencing severe tension because her work conflicts with her personal values. Once Liz has identified this, she can make a decision about what to do to relieve her stress. She can:

- **remove the stressor**: this might mean renegotiating her position at work, or even working for a different company;
- **change her attitude to the stressor**: this might mean assessing just how strongly she feels about the issue, and if necessary finding a different way of looking at the work.

ACTIVITY 19: Assess your options

Apply this process to situations that you find stressful.

- What is causing me stress?
- Can I remove the stressor?
- Can I reduce the stressor?
- Can I change my way of thinking about it?
- What can I learn to do differently?
- What skills do I need to develop in order to do this?

Develop your interpersonal skills

Although you can change only yourself, and not somebody else, the way that you behave and communicate will influence the way that others perceive you and behave towards you. Start by identifying just what it is about the relationship or situation that you find stressful, then decide how best to tackle it. This will involve expressing your feelings in an appropriate way and to the right person.

Scene 22: Kristina's boss

Kristina complains constantly about her boss, Julie. Julie is demanding and unpredictable, she says, and has no sense of humour. Kristina knows that this situation is getting her down, and decides to do something about it. She works out what is the aspect of Julie's behaviour that causes her most stress, and realizes that it is the way that Julie changes her mind about what she wants halfway through a project, and doesn't communicate the new details right away. Kristina thinks, 'That's it – but what can I do about it?'

Kristina could learn how to communicate assertively. She could discuss the situation with Julie, tell her how difficult she finds this particular situation and ask Julie to keep her informed in the future.

Scene 23: *Adrienne is bored and frustrated*

When Adrienne joined the graduate scheme she hoped for stimulating and interesting work. However, she finds that she is doing repetitive administrative tasks, and feels tense and demotivated. Adrienne feels that the only way out of this situation is to leave and look for a more interesting job, but that would mean breaking her contract. She finds this a very stressful situation.

'It's getting to me so much that I'm starting to make silly mistakes in the work I am doing,' she confides in her mother. 'And I get a tension headache every day.'

'Talk to the right person about this,' her mother advises. 'Explain how you feel, and ask when you can expect more interesting work.'

Adrienne is horrified. 'I can't do that! It would seem like being pushy!'

'No it wouldn't. It means being assertive, that's all. The first thing you could do is find out how to develop that skill, and practise.'

Adrienne follows this advice, and has a discussion with her line manager. What emerges is that the work she is doing at the moment is to familiarize herself with different aspects of the department, and that she will shortly move on to more challenging work.

'I'm glad I brought it up,' Adrienne tells her mother. 'I feel better for having said what I was feeling, and it has opened up communication with my manager.'

If Adrienne had received a less encouraging response, she would still be in a better position to make a firm decision about her future.

ACTIVITY 20: Which interpersonal skills should I develop?

Choose three situations in which gaining the outcome you desire depends on using interpersonal skills. In each case, identify the type of communication that is required.

Situation	Outcome I want	Type of skill to develop
Feeling angry with team members who take long breaks	Them to take shorter breaks, and us to maintain a good relationship	Requesting a change in behaviour

1 _____

2 _____

3 _____

_____

Assertive behaviour

Behaving assertively is a good way of managing stress. This kind of behaviour helps you to maintain some control over your thoughts, feelings and actions. You will find the skills of assertion particularly helpful when it comes to refusing requests and asking for what you want, and behaving assertively also prevents the build-up of stressful situations by enabling you to express your feelings appropriately.

Assertive behaviour is based on:

- respecting yourself;
- respecting other people;
- knowing what you feel about a situation and what outcome you would like;
- communicating honestly, directly and appropriately.

Other types of behaviour

Don't think that communicating assertively means that you will always get what you want or get your own way. If your goal is to come out on top you are demonstrating an aggressive attitude rather than an assertive approach. Aggressive behaviour is based on the determination to win and dominate, and does not respect or acknowledge the rights of the other person. At the other extreme, people who behave passively or submissively indicate that they feel that they have no rights and that others may impose on them or dominate them.

How to recognize aggressive behaviour

Some types of aggression are easily spotted. Shouting, pointing, towering over you, coming too close are examples of behaviour that is threatening and aggressive and can cause the recipient to feel scared and helpless.

Other types of aggression are more subtle. Speaking very quietly can be an aggressive strategy, as can an over-friendly tone of voice or body language. Pretending to be friendly is one way of manipulating the recipients into believing that they are being acknowledged and respected. In fact, the person who behaves like this is intent on getting his or her own way by indirect means. Other examples which may fall into this category include practices such as dropping hints or pretending that you are speaking on someone else's behalf. Experiencing this kind of behaviour can make us feel manipulated and used.

How to recognize submissive behaviour

Submissive or passive behaviour gives the message that you will take whatever is doled out to you. Not asking for what you want, not expressing feelings or opinions, being unable to say no to a request are characteristics of this kind of behaviour. A quiet, uncertain tone of voice, fidgety mannerisms, reluctance to look others in the eye are some indications of passive behaviour, which seems to say to the world, 'I have no rights as a person. You can walk all over me. I will take it.' Dealing with someone who behaves submissively can be baffling and frustrating. You may find yourself responding in ways you don't like: for example, perhaps feeling forced to take control and make decisions when you are not sure of the other person's thoughts and feelings.

There are some behaviours which may seem to be passive, but are in fact a subtle form of aggression. Silence is one of these. When someone refuses to respond, or avoids speaking to you, this 'silent treatment' may be seen as aggressive. The person is using silence as a blunt weapon to make you feel uncomfortable. Again, you may feel manipulated and angry when you are at the receiving end of this kind of behaviour.

How to deal with aggressive, submissive and manipulative behaviour

Your instinct might be to meet aggression with aggression, maybe thinking that this will show that you will not be trampled on. When you are faced with passive or manipulative behaviour, you may fall into the 'two can play at that game' trap and use the same tactics yourself, or you might find that your frustration leads you to respond angrily and aggressively.

The best way of responding to these kinds of behaviour is to be assertive. Assertion involves standing up for your rights in a way that does not infringe the rights of others. It means taking responsibility for yourself, acknowledging the way that you think, feel and behave, and communicating directly with other people, without pretence or game-playing. You listen to what people say, and ask questions and give feedback constructively. You are prepared to compromise.

How to behave assertively

Step 1: Decide what you feel and what outcome you want

Think about the point of your communication. Identify exactly what it is you want to discuss and what you want to happen. Be as specific as you can. Do you want to reach an agreement? Do you want to be offered something? Do you just want to have an exchange of views?

Step 2: Choose the time and place for the encounter

Think about the nature of the discussion. Should it take place in private or within earshot of other people? One of the golden rules of effective communication is to praise in public and criticize in private. Choose your timing. How are you and the other person likely to feel? How long should the discussion be? If the issue is significant you might choose a time when neither of you will have an eye on the clock. Timing will affect the way in which you make it clear that your working relationship will not be damaged by the fact that you have, say, refused a request for help, or reprimanded someone. If there is a long gap between the meeting and your next interaction, it may be tricky to re-establish normal communication.

Step 3: Recognize the feelings/position of the other person

Acknowledge that you have some degree of empathy for the other person's situation: 'I realize that you thought it was funny'; 'I know that you have strong views on this matter'; 'I understand that you are under pressure from ...'; 'I know you want me to ...'

Step 4: Make a clear statement of your position and say what you would like to happen

This could be an expression of your thoughts or feelings, or an explanation of the situation:

'I don't find it amusing.'

'I want us to go ahead with the programme.'

'I am not confident about taking this on at the moment.'

Adjust the level of your disclosure to suit the situation. At work, you might wish not to place as much emphasis on your personal feelings as you would in a private life situation. For example, instead of saying, 'I felt so embarrassed when you contradicted me in front of the customer', you could say, 'I found myself in an embarrassing position when ...'

Step 5: Suggest the specific action to be taken

Make clear what you want to happen. The strength of your expression here depends on the situation. In some cases, you will want to be quite prescriptive, while at other times you may wish to say that you want to work out a joint solution, or reach a compromise.

Step 6: Listen to the response

Pay attention to what the other person says. Listen for the whole meaning. Pay attention to body language. If someone's words and behaviour seem to contradict each other, focus on what the behaviour is telling you.

Step 7: Check your understanding of the response

Ask questions to make sure that you have understood the other person's position. Use paraphrasing to show that you have listened and to check that you have got it right:

'So you think that it is unfair that . . .'

'So what you would like to happen is . . .'

'As you see it . . .'

Step 8: Encourage discussion

Open up discussion with phrases such as 'How could we . . .?' In many situations you will want to reach a compromise. In these cases, show that you are open-minded and that you want to include the other person in negotiations.

Step 9: Restate your case

You might need to do this if the person ignores what you are saying or brings in irrelevant matters. You repeat your main point and do not allow yourself to be distracted or side-tracked:

'I know that other people . . . but we're talking about . . .'

'I realize that it is not a requirement in every department, but . . .'

'I know that we are under pressure to complete the order, but I . . .'

Step 10: Try to reach an agreement

The important thing is that at the end of the conversation you are both clear about what has been said and what happens next.

You can put these guidelines into practice in all work situations. You can adapt them to suit particular circumstances and you can vary the kind of wording you use, but if you follow the basic principles of assertive communication you will deal effectively with potentially stressful situations and you will establish and develop positive working relationships.

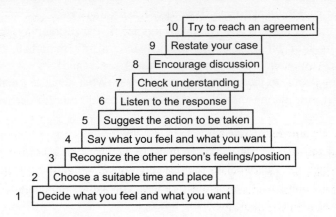

10	Try to reach an agreement
9	Restate your case
8	Encourage discussion
7	Check understanding
6	Listen to the response
5	Suggest the action to be taken
4	Say what you feel and what you want
3	Recognize the other person's feelings/position
2	Choose a suitable time and place
1	Decide what you feel and what you want

Figure 3 Ten steps to assertion

Scene 24: Bob's day off

Bob wants to have a day off so that he can travel to his friend's wedding. It is a very busy time at work, and they are short-staffed. He decides that the best time to approach Lorna about this is just before lunch. It's a bit risky, he thinks, because she might be hungry or preoccupied with what she has to do at lunch time, but then again, if her initial reaction is negative, he can ask her to use the break to consider his request further.

Bob begins by acknowledging Lorna's situation and expressing his feelings. 'I know this is a really busy time for us and that we are two staff short, and so I feel a bit embarrassed asking, but I would like to have Friday off.'

Lorna has had a fraught morning and is feeling under pressure. Her instinctive reaction is to tell him he can forget it. However, she does not reply immediately. She always finds it a helpful strategy to pause for a few seconds before responding, to give her time to consider her response. She uses neutral phrases such as, 'Right, let me think,' or repeats what has been said: 'So what you're asking is . . .' This enables her to respond calmly. On this occasion she says, 'Have I got this clear, Bob? You want to take next Friday off?'

'That's right,' says Bob. 'I can see that you don't like the idea, but it is important to me. I wouldn't ask otherwise.'

Lorna shows that she has taken this in. 'I realize you wouldn't ask for time off right at this moment if it wasn't important, but we're very stretched, as you know, and I really need you.'

Bob opens up the negotiation a bit more. 'What about if I make up the time during the following week? I could come in early or stay late.'

Lorna now has to use her judgement. She has moved on from her initial negative response and can think about what Bob is asking and what he is offering. Each of them is behaving assertively. No matter what the outcome, they have communicated clearly, and neither has tried to manipulate or push the other.

Situations in which assertive communication can reduce stress

Confident, appropriate communication can significantly reduce the anxiety and tension we experience when we feel under pressure in particular situations. It is also the pathway to improving relationships and to sorting out task-related issues. It will help you when:

- your workload is too heavy;
- you are unclear about aspects of your role and responsibilities;
- you are given a deadline that you think is unrealistic;
- someone's behaviour is causing you distress or concern;
- you want to ask for something – a change in your working practice, more training, etc.

Saying no and keeping your job

One of the basic principles that assertive communication supports is our right to say no. At the same time, remember that having this right does not mean that you are obliged to exercise it. There will be times when you would like to say no to something or someone, but choose to say yes. The key word here is 'choose'. Making a considered choice is different from feeling intimidated or pushed into a corner. However, think carefully about how you usually respond. If you find it difficult to say no to requests to do more work, or to help people out, or to work to unrealistic deadlines, and are frequently taking on extra tasks or doing things for other people when you would prefer not to, the build-up of resentment and frustration can be very stressful. Here are some suggestions about how to say no to people without damaging your career prospects!

Make it clear

Make your refusal clear but polite. You do not need to apologize, but there is no harm in using a phrase like 'I'm sorry' – it tends to come out automatically anyway, and in this context is more a form of verbal politeness signifying vague regret than an actual apology. Giving a reason, not an excuse, helps to maintain good relationships. You are refusing the request, not rejecting the person. An example of a good reason for refusing a request is that doing what is being asked would prevent you from doing your present work effectively and to the required standard.

Say 'No, but . . .'

Where possible, say what you *can* do. 'I can't help you sort out the stock now, but I could help when I've finished this report.' This response shows that you are not refusing the request outright and opens up negotiation.

Make constructive suggestions

You could follow your refusal with some suggestions about how the task could be done in a different way or by someone else, or you could describe the circumstances in which you would be able to agree: 'I could do that if we . . .'

It is a good idea to include others, especially your boss, in considering ways in which you might be able to do what is being asked. You might say something like, 'I would like to help with that, but it would mean putting something off. What thoughts do you have about the way round this?'

Listen to your thoughts as well as your feelings

Your gut reaction might be to say no to something: for example, a task that is not strictly within your remit and which you know you have a right to refuse. However, ask yourself if doing the task would in fact help you to achieve any of your work goals.

Dealing with criticism the stress-free way

Having to give or receive criticism or negative feedback can be a difficult experience that puts you under great pressure. Situations that can be hard to handle confidently and effectively include:

- having to criticize a friend;
- a newly promoted manager or supervisor having to reprimand a former team colleague;
- being criticized unfairly.

Your own ideas:

_____

_____

Reasons why we find criticism hard to handle include:

- feeling inadequate;
- feeling that we are being attacked unfairly;
- feeling that only our negative aspects are noticed;
- feeling that giving negative feedback will cause us to be disliked;
- feeling humiliated;
- feeling that we are being put on the defensive.

Your own ideas:

_____

_____

You can learn to deal positively with criticism. It is never pleasant to receive negative comments, but you can prepare yourself for this by becoming aware of your areas of weakness at work. What you do about any faults is up to you – you can choose to live with them, or you can take steps to improve them. Either way, you accept that it is possible that on occasion your behaviour may be criticized, and that you can respond to the criticism confidently and appropriately.

On the receiving end

Do not react immediately. Consciously relax your body, and listen to what is being said. If you are totally taken aback, ask for time to think about it before you respond. If you are following the guidelines for assertive communication, you could begin by acknowledging the criticism and expressing your feelings. 'You're saying that I didn't pull my weight when . . . I feel really surprised to hear that. I need to take some time to think it over.'

Think about how true the criticism is. If it is a valid comment which you know to be true, the best thing to do is acknowledge it, apologize if you think it is appropriate to do so, and show that you are prepared to make any changes to prevent it happening again. If you feel that there are circumstances which might be taken into account, explain what they are after you have accepted the criticism, and make sure that you offer them as an explanation, not an excuse. 'I agree that I was behind in delivering those materials. I'm sorry about the problems that the late delivery caused. I think I should look at the way I prioritize my work.'

If you disagree with what has been said, show that you have listened to the point, then say that you don't agree, and say why. Watch your body language – keep calm and relaxed, and try to speak in steady, even tones. You might want to ask for more information. You could say something like 'I'm surprised that you should think I was rude on the phone. I don't agree – I think I was firm and polite. What did I do or say that made you see it differently?' In this case, you might get some useful feedback about your communication style, or the person offering the criticism, having failed to think through exactly what point he or she wanted to make, will have to back down.

If you agree with part of what has been said, accept that element of the comment, but question the part that you disagree with. 'I agree that my work has been not so accurate recently, but it is not true that I always make mistakes.'

Some useful phrases that take the heat out of the situation:

I can see that it may seem that way to you.

This expression plays safe by showing that you acknowledge what has been said, but do not want to be drawn into a discussion about it. It is also a way of not engaging with criticism. This response is particularly useful when you are faced with what you feel is more a manipulative put-down than a genuine criticism.

I agree, I am not good at checking the final details/your own example.

This response disarms your critic. By calmly agreeing with what has been said you cut short the exchange.

Scene 25: Gareth listens to criticism

Gareth's boss Trevor says to him, 'I think you have become very negative in your attitude. It seems as if you are not a team player any more.'

Gareth feels as if he has been kicked. His heart starts to race and he feels his blood pounding in his head. His instinct is to lash out at Trevor and tell him that he's talking a load of rubbish.

Instead, Gareth controls himself. He breathes slowly and regularly, and gets the tension out of his shoulders and jaw. As he does so he thinks about what Trevor has said. He replies, 'To tell you the truth, I don't know what to say to that. I don't think my work or attitude has changed. What makes you think that it has?'

Trevor says, 'Well, you didn't make much of a contribution when we were planning how to cope with the new legislation.'

Gareth thinks about this. 'That's probably true. I feel pretty annoyed about yet more stuff being imposed on us. But I am as committed to the team as I always have been. I am surprised that you should think anything different.'

The discussion can continue in a calm and reasonable way. Gareth's handling of the criticism turns a potentially stressful and unsatisfactory exchange into a positive and helpful encounter.

Giving criticism

The phrase 'giving criticism' covers a range of situations. It could refer to times when you have to reprimand someone for unacceptable behaviour, such as poor time-keeping or work that is below standard. It could refer to occasions when you want to point out the negative effect that someone's behaviour is having on you or on other people. Whatever the situation, giving criticism assertively is an excellent way of dealing with people you find difficult and whose behaviour contributes to your stress.

Scene 26: Lizzie has to reprimand one of her former team

Lizzie has recently been promoted, and is now manager of the small team she used to be part of. She notices that Sanjay has started to take very frequent cigarette breaks, and she knows that she must take the matter up with him. Lizzie feels embarrassed because until recently they were working alongside each other, and Sanjay will know about times when she herself stretched the rules. She does not like Sanjay's attitude, and feels that he is taking advantage of the situation.

Step 1: Identify specifically the behaviour you want to criticize

The first thing that Lizzie does is to identify precisely the behaviour that she wishes to criticize. She knows that criticism should be based on specific behaviour that can be observed, so she puts her feelings about Sanjay's attitude and motives to the back of her mind and focuses on the issue in hand, which is the number and length of breaks he takes.

Lizzie also decides to disclose that she feels embarrassed and that the situation is an awkward one. Sharing her feelings in this way is positive and assertive.

Step 2: Choose the time and place

Lizzie decides to speak to Sanjay just before the morning break. She wants the discussion to be private, but in this case does not want to call Sanjay to her office. She decides to tell Sanjay she wants to talk something over with him, and asks him to walk along to the canteen with her.

Step 3: Introduce the topic and describe the behaviour that you want to change
Lizzie begins by saying, 'Sanjay, I want to talk to you about the breaks you are taking. I don't like doing this, because we always worked well together and I know you are a valuable team member.' She goes on to describe the nature of the breaks that she has observed Sanjay taking.

Remember to describe the behaviour, and not to evaluate or judge the person. Stick to just one point. Avoid the temptation to bring in other matters that occur to you.

Step 4: Ask for a specific change
Lizzie is careful to be very clear about what behaviour she would like to see in the future. If she uses vague words like 'fewer' or 'shorter' she is leaving the situation too open.

In asking for the change, do acknowledge the other person's situation or feelings. Say that you understand if the person has been under a lot of pressure, for example, or that you know that he or she has always been used to doing things in a certain way.

Step 5: Get a response to what you have said
Lizzie says to Sanjay, 'That's the situation as I see it. What do you think about what I've said?'

Sanjay shrugs and says, 'Wendy takes the same number of breaks.'

Lizzie acknowledges what he has said, and restates her case (see 'How to behave assertively', p. 58). She says, 'That may be so, but at the moment we are talking about what *you* do.'

Remember that the other person has a right to accept or reject your criticism (within the understood or contractual job specifications). Show that you are willing to discuss the issue and that you are listening to the response. A good way of encouraging discussion is to ask about what kind of time scale would be suitable. Sanjay should be able to do what is required immediately; for other situations, you could ask what the person thinks would be a reasonable time in which a change may be seen to have taken place – a week? a month?

Step 6: Specify positive and negative consequences
Sanjay accepts what Lizzie says and agrees to change his behaviour,

and Lizzie does not think that she needs to point out what may happen if he does not do as she asks. Instead she highlights the positive and says, 'Great. I'm sure we will all benefit from a more focused working atmosphere.'

You may need to point out the negative consequences if the required action does not take place. In certain cases you may need to say that you will have to take the matter further if there is no change. In these situations, make clear that you regret having to point out such consequences and, where possible, indicate that you expect a positive outcome and that you are sure your warning is unnecessary.

Step 7: Encourage discussion about the issue

Discussion may not be necessary if the situation is cut and dried, but you may wish to look at ways of bringing about the change you have requested, or of reaching a compromise about it. Ask the other person for suggestions, so that there is a sense of involvement and control on both sides.

Step 8: Finish the conversation

Summarize what has been agreed. You should both understand what has been said and what is required.

One way of finishing on a positive note is to offer a 'sandwich' – the criticism is the filling between two slices of praise. You start with a good comment, then give the necessary criticism, ending with something pleasant and upbeat. Two points to bear in mind, however:

1 If you use this technique too frequently it becomes stale and routine, so try to vary the delivery while honouring the concepts.
2 Resist the temptation to follow your positive opening with the word 'but'. Just leave it out, so that your initial comment has weight and stands by itself. 'But' has the effect of cancelling the favourable comment. You do not need to say it – show the shift in the conversation with your tone of voice and body language.

The benefits of constructive criticism

Giving and receiving criticism assertively increases your respect for yourself and others. Communicating your views in this way turns situations which might be stressful into opportunities for personal and professional growth. This kind of behaviour helps to value and promote positive working relationships. Feedback which is based on appropriate and honest communication, stemming from a desire to improve a situation, leads to a positive working environment in which feelings and situations are faced and dealt with rather than left to fester or to become the source of anger, resentment and aggression.

ACTIVITY 21: Behaving assertively

Choose three situations in which you would like to behave assertively. Plan what you will say and how you will behave.

Situation	What I will say	How I will say it
1		
2		
3		

Dealing with a bully

Recognizing bullying behaviour

Bullying is not just a problem associated with school playgrounds. It is an adult issue which affects thousands of people in the workplace. The type of bullying behaviour experienced includes constant faultfinding over trivial issues, destructive criticism, even physical aggression such as intimidating body language or slaps or punches. Sometimes psychological ploys will be used, such as isolating the victim from supportive colleagues, or spreading rumours about his or her ability to do the job. Another tactic is to make sure that the victim will fail – for example, by setting him or her up with difficult projects and very few resources.

It is no consolation for targets of bullies to know that the perpetrator tends to be weak and insecure, using these tactics as a way of exerting power and gaining control. Bullies often display manipulative behaviour, covering their real intention with a charming and plausible manner. Often they will finish with one victim and move on to another – more than 90 per cent of the reported incidents of workplace bullying are caused by this kind of 'serial' bully.

What you can do

1 Don't be prepared to suffer in silence. Collect your facts. Keep a log or diary of every incident. Make a note of any witnesses. Talk to colleagues about what is going on.
2 Depending on the nature and level of the bullying behaviour, you could deal with the person directly. Using the assertive approach described above, you could state clearly that you are aware of what is happening and that you want it to stop. If you are unable to confront the bully directly, you could speak to your line manager or human resource department about the problem.
3 If the above approaches do not work, you could consider taking legal action. Your professional organization may warn you that this is a last resort. Laws against harassment and discrimination provide a lever for dealing with bullying based on these factors, but it is harder to bring a case against more general victimization, as there is as yet no legislation about the specific issue of workplace bullying.
4 You may be left with no option other than to remove yourself from the stressor by finding another job or getting a transfer to a department where you will have no contact with the bully. You may feel that this is letting someone get away with threatening behaviour, but at the same time, making a decision to protect yourself and to enable yourself to work free from fear and intimidation is a positive step which will enhance your well-being.

Change the way that you work

The way that you manage your workload may be a source of stress. You might feel that you have too much to do, or that you cannot cope with certain aspects of your job. Skills you could develop include elements of time management such as prioritizing or delegating. You also might consider whether you would benefit from further training or updating in particular areas of your job.

Whichever strategies you choose are likely to be linked with interpersonal communication. For example, changing the way that you manage your workload may well involve learning to say no to requests. It could also involve learning how to make requests, for more training, for example, or for the opportunity to work flexi-hours or from home.

ACTIVITY 22: Skills for managing your workload

Identify three areas in which gaining the outcome you desire depends on developing different skills.

Situation	Outcome I want	Type of skill to be developed
Feeling over-whelmed by too much work	To manage my workload so that I feel more in control	Prioritizing Saying no
1		
2		
3		

Stress-free ways of dealing with your workload

Managing time

If you manage your time effectively you will not only reduce your stress levels, but you will work more productively, be able to experience more pleasure and enjoyment from your work and create opportunities for a wider range of activities. Time management is not about packing more activities into an already crowded day, but is about deciding how you want to use this most precious commodity. All too often we find that the day is over and we have not done what we intended to do, or achieved anything really significant.

The keys to managing time are **setting goals, prioritizing** and **planning.**

Know your work goals
Your work goals are your overview of what you want to achieve. In the pressure of the working week it can be easy to lose sight of the big picture and see only a series of tasks that have to be done. Once you have decided what you want to accomplish in your working life, both in the short term and in the long term, you have a focus for your activities.

ACTIVITY 23: Identifying work goals

1 Begin by brainstorming everything you can think of. Just write the ideas down as they come into your head.

2 Turn each idea into a concrete statement. Vague goals such as to be 'earning more money', 'working in media', 'in a position of responsibility', 'working from home' or 'better at dealing with difficult people and situations' are less helpful than ones which give a specific description. Make it short and concise: 'To be heading a telesales team', 'To be working in the Paris office', 'To be earning £xxxxx'.

3 Now separate the ideas into short-term and long-term goals. For each, decide how much time you will give yourself. A goal without a deadline loses much of its value.

What I want to achieve	*Short-term time scale*	*Long-term time scale*
1		
2		
3		

4 _____

5 _____

6 _____

_____

Assess your work goals

This process will have helped you to see which of your goals are realistic and achievable. If you cannot express a goal in concrete terms, with a specific time scale, it is probably an indication that it is just a vague idea that you play with now and then, but do not really intend to pursue. Writing down a goal is a vital step in making it happen – it turns an abstract thought into something real.

Assess your motivation

Think about your reason for planning to achieve particular aims. If your goals are not linked to your work values and what you want from work, then it is possible that you are channelling your energies in the wrong direction. Remember that your motivation and aims are personal to you. It can be easy to get side-tracked by the expectations of other people and the culture of the organization. For example, the next obvious step for you might be to aim for promotion to team leader or manager. However, check to see if this goal fits your needs.

ACTIVITY 24: Check your motivation

For each goal, write down why you want to achieve it. If the reason is inappropriate or irrelevant to your overall work aims, cross out the goal.

Goal   Why I want to achieve it

1 _____

2 _____

3 _____

4 _____

5 _____

6 _____

Scene 27: Chloe assesses her motivation

Chloe has been in her present position for a few years, and the next obvious step is to apply for a managerial post. Her line manager encourages her, and her co-workers assume that she will climb the career ladder in this way. However, when Chloe thinks about this goal, she realizes that she is being influenced by what others expect of her. A role as a manager in her workplace will give her less hands-on work and will remove her from everyday contact with people, aspects of her job which she finds very satisfying, and will give her more paperwork, which she does not enjoy. Chloe realizes that what she wants to achieve is to further develop her personal and practical skills.

Is the goal still relevant?

Your work goals are not written in stone – they can change. When you formulate a goal you are declaring your intention to achieve it, and there is no point in working to achieve something which you no longer want or is no longer feasible. What was a relevant aim a few years or even months ago may not be so now. Once you have written down your goals, check them frequently and be prepared to adjust them or get rid of them. The process of reviewing your goals and making fresh ones is a way of reminding yourself of what you have achieved and keeping you focused on what matters to you.

Does the goal contribute to a balanced life?

Check to see how your work goals fit into your life goals (more about this in Chapter 5). Watch out for any clashes or areas of potential conflict.

Scene 28: Lewis changes direction

Lewis has always aimed to start up his own business. However, he knows that doing so will involve him in working long and erratic hours, often away from home. Lewis now has a young family, and he really wants to be home for at least two evenings a week and to be with them at the weekends. Lewis decides that working for himself is not a good option for him at the moment.

Plan to achieve your goals

Write down a plan for each goal. Break them down into tasks which will help you to achieve your aim. Break down each task into segments.

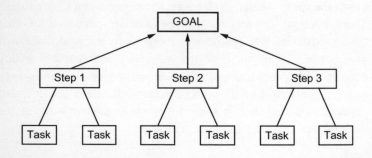

Figure 4 Goal and activity diagram

How to prioritize

Prioritizing is a matter of deciding what should come first. It means keeping an eye on your main work objectives and being realistic about what you can achieve. Being clear about what is urgent, what is important and what can wait helps you to plan your activities and gives you a sense of being in control.

Urgent v. important

Sometimes everything seems so urgent that you do not know where to begin, and you may end up making your decision based on such factors as who asks in the most demanding way, or doing first something that isn't important or urgent but which you like doing. When this happens, take a minute to think about what really needs to be done first. Importance and urgency are not the same thing.

Something is important if:

- it is of high value in relation to your goals;
- it is of high value in relation to your key tasks;
- it will have a long-term effect on you and your working life.

Something is urgent if:

- it has to be done to meet a deadline.

Do not think that something's urgency is necessarily related to its importance. You have to do the urgent tasks, but you should also give a high priority to important items, particularly those which will help you to achieve your goals.

ACTIVITY 25: Prioritizing

Make a list of all the tasks that you intend to accomplish tomorrow. Place them in the time square below.

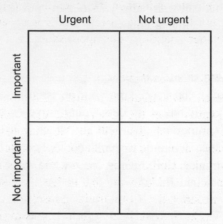

Figure 5 Time square

How to use your time square

This square helps you to identify what you should do first. You can number each item according to its priority, based on the above definitions of important and urgent.

The most important square and the one which is often overlooked is the Important, 'Not urgent block. These are the activities related to the goals which matter most to you. For example, to achieve your aim you might need to get a qualification, or to establish a network of contacts, or to become more confident in dealing with people. Because you do not have an externally imposed deadline for these activities, it is easy to keep putting them off. Make sure that this time square contains steps that will help you to fulfil your aims. If you do this you maintain the element of control and direction which will sustain you in times of pressure.

Move items around the square, and be prepared to drop anything which remains not important and not urgent.

Time and your working style

The way that you manage tasks and your workload is to a large extent influenced by your personality. Your personal preferences and the factors that motivate you affect your approach to organizing your workload and using the available time. Your preferred way of working is likely to be a strength when the level of pressure is right for you and you are not feeling under stress, but if your stress level rises, you could consider adapting your approach.

Scene 29: Working to a deadline

Colin and Leah each have deadlines to meet in a month's time. Colin plans backwards from the given date, allocating time to work on aspects of the job that will enable him to meet the deadline comfortably and to allow time for unexpected hitches. Working like this makes Colin feel in control. The pressure of the deadline is manageable, and knowing that he has the task in hand lets him work to his strengths. Colin prides himself on producing accurate, reliable work. He finds it stressful if he has to rush to get something finished, and does not do his best work in those circumstances.

Although Colin leaves plenty of time for completing a task, his focus on accuracy and perfection means that he sometimes does become stressed about getting work finished not only in time but also to his exacting standards.

Leah, on the other hand, works best when she is under a lot of pressure. She likes feeling that she has to go all out to beat the clock, and enjoys the adrenaline rush that helps her to keep going. The challenge of having to produce something in a very limited space of time sharpens her mind and brings out her ability to work quickly and effectively.

Leah's preference for working quickly in short bursts of energy means that she does tend to make mistakes, and she does not allow time for checking and putting things right. Sometimes Leah finds that the level of pressure she imposes on herself stops being enjoyable and becomes stressful.

Colin's and Leah's working styles are totally unalike. Each of them may benefit from adopting certain aspects of the other's style. Colin could consider whether his passion for accuracy is always justified, and he might decide, where appropriate, to sacrifice perfection for speed of delivery; Leah could adopt some aspects of Colin's methodical approach, and plan her work in stages so that she has to meet interim deadlines.

Once you are aware of your preferred working style, you can assess how it affects your time management, and use your knowledge to help you to manage the pressure of demands and deadlines. It is most likely that you have a mixture of styles, with one strong pattern of behaviour and some examples of behaviour from one or more other categories.

The following exercises will help you to identify and explore four styles of working and their effect on your time management.

ACTIVITY 26: Are you a perfectionist?

	True	Partly true	Not true
1 I like things to be 100 per cent right	☐	☐	☐
2 I check facts thoroughly	☐	☐	☐
3 I prepare down to the last detail	☐	☐	☐
4 I do everything myself, so that I know it's done properly	☐	☐	☐

Advantages of this style
Your strengths are your attention to detail and your highly developed planning skills. Your work is accurate and well organized, and you think ahead, anticipating problems and building in contingency plans.

Disadvantages of this style
Your concern for detail might lead to you being unable to see the wood for the trees. You may give too much information without identifying what is really important. You probably set yourself

unrealistically high standards, and expect the same from others. This may lead to you being critical of your co-workers because they do not live up to your requirements, and could stop you from delegating, since you do not trust anyone else to do the job well. It is possible that because you want to get it right, you spend too much time and energy in planning.

Stress-reducing tips for perfectionists
Learn to prioritize.
Set realistic standards.
Monitor the amount of planning time that you schedule.
Monitor the amount of information you provide.
Become tolerant of others' mistakes.
Set yourself deadlines, e.g. 'I will give myself 15 minutes to do this.'
Learn to delegate.
Learn to identify what is 'good enough' and accept it.
Avoid perfection on things which are not central.
Estimate how much time tasks and projects are really worth.
Prioritize different aspects of a task to keep you focused on what is essential.

ACTIVITY 27: Do you enjoy the rush?

	True	Partly true	Not true
1 I achieve a lot in a little time	☐	☐	☐
2 I enjoy working in short bursts	☐	☐	☐
3 I like having lots of things to do	☐	☐	☐
4 I like starting something at the last minute	☐	☐	☐
5 I like having new challenges	☐	☐	☐
6 I like getting projects off the ground	☐	☐	☐
7 I don't like routine work	☐	☐	☐

Advantages of this style
You can get a lot done in a short space of time, and you can maintain a fresh and enthusiastic approach. You love new activities and relish taking on challenges. You are at your best when you are under pressure, such as having a tight deadline (the more seemingly impossible the better), or are in the presence of people you want to impress. You are also good at discovering time-saving ways of working and getting things done.

Disadvantages of this style
You may skip the necessary preparation for a task, and in your haste you tend to make mistakes and not check your work. It is likely that you steam ahead without gathering enough information, and so make poor decisions. Leaving too much until the last minute puts a strain on you and the people with whom you work. You might be easily distracted by more interesting topics.

Stress-busting tips for hurriers
Plan your work in stages.
Plan time for preparing as well as for the task itself.
When you plan a task, include all aspects.
Work backwards from final deadlines.
Build in a buffer zone to deal with things that go wrong.
Learn to apply slowdown and relaxation techniques.
Take time to listen to what people say.
Make realistic time estimates.
Think before you take on something new.

ACTIVITY 28: Are you a people pleaser?

	True	Partly true	Not true
1 I like being part of a team	☐	☐	☐
2 I am aware of others' feelings	☐	☐	☐
3 I don't like upsetting people	☐	☐	☐
4 I let people interrupt me	☐	☐	☐

Advantages of this style
Your skill with people means that you can form and develop positive working relationships. You are good at teamwork and building morale, and you value people's feelings. You bring sensitivity and intuition to your dealings with your co-workers, and create an atmosphere of mutual help and collaboration.

Disadvantages of this style
You may well find it difficult to give criticism or to disagree. It is likely that you dislike refusing requests for help, or asking people to wait, and that you take on too much work. You could spend too much time in consultation and getting feedback, and shy away from making decisions.

Stress-busting tips for people pleasers
    Learn to say no.
    Learn to give criticism appropriately.
    Learn to prioritize.
    Don't rely on your feelings and intuition – ask questions and find out what is required.
    Learn to make requests and ask for what you want.

ACTIVITY 29: Are you a tower of strength?

	True	Partly true	Not true
1 I like being strong and competent in a crisis	☐	☐	☐
2 I stay calm, no matter what	☐	☐	☐
3 I have a strong sense of duty	☐	☐	☐
4 I dislike asking for help	☐	☐	☐

Advantages of this style
You stay calm and rational even when you are under great pressure – in fact, your strengths emerge when there is a crisis. You can take control of a situation and deal calmly with people who may be panicking or flapping. You take on unpleasant tasks and deal with matters firmly and fairly. It is likely that you are quick-thinking and look for the logical, practical solution to a problem.

Disadvantages of this style
Possibly you feel uncomfortable revealing or admitting weakness, and you may dislike asking for help. Your way of coping may make you appear distant and unemotional. The fact that others know that they can rely on you and the fact that you may pride yourself on your ability to cope could lead to you taking on too much.

Stress-busting tips for towers of strength
Check requirements of tasks before taking them on.
Learn to ask for help.
Monitor your workload.
Learn to delegate.

Common time problems

Procrastination

The word 'procrastination' comes from the Latin word *cras*, which means 'tomorrow'. It refers to the practice of leaving things until tomorrow, or a later date. Many of us put off doing unpleasant, demanding or tedious tasks, often discovering that the consequences of doing this are far more stressful than tackling the job in the first place.

Scene 30: Fran puts it off

Fran has to prepare sales figures for the annual report. She dislikes this part of her job, but knows that it has to be done. 'I'll deal with those figures first thing tomorrow morning,' she tells herself. However, when she sits down at her desk the next morning she thinks it is so untidy that she must clear it up before she can start working. When the desk top is clear and the plant has been watered she remembers that she ought to phone Sandra to wish her a good holiday. When that conversation is over Fran thinks, 'I might as well check my emails before I start, so that I won't be distracted by wondering what messages I've got.' She spends some time replying to emails, and looks at one or two items of junk mail that might be amusing. 'I'll just get a cup of coffee before I start,' she thinks. She sips her coffee and looks at the newly watered plant. 'Those leaves look a bit drab. I'll nip out and get some of that leaf-shine stuff.' When a friend phones later in the morning Fran moans, 'You've no idea how busy I am. I've got to do the sales figures – it's a huge job and it takes up all my time. They just don't realize what a strain it is.'

Fran's behaviour illustrates some of the ways in which we put off, and justify putting off, things that we don't want to do. Her tension eases as she engages in the unimportant activities that she does instead of what she should be doing, but her stress levels rise dramatically when she realizes that she has even less time in which to complete her task.

ACTIVITY 30: Are you a procrastinator?

Check the descriptions that apply to you.

	Yes	Sometimes	No
Do you find that you let your mind wander?	☐	☐	☐
Do you welcome interruptions?	☐	☐	☐
Are you easily distracted by other tasks?	☐	☐	☐
Do you frequently say things like, 'I'll just do one more thing before I start?'	☐	☐	☐
Do you find that you 'have to' read and reply to emails as they arrive?	☐	☐	☐

Do you find that you 'have to' read and reply to text messages as they arrive?	☐	☐	☐
Do you take frequent food or drink breaks?	☐	☐	☐
Do you keep finding 'good' reasons for not starting something?	☐	☐	☐
Do you need to have every piece of information to hand before you start a task?	☐	☐	☐
Do you talk a lot about how much you have to do?	☐	☐	☐

Add your own ideas

_____	☐	☐	☐
_____	☐	☐	☐

Why we put things off

The first step in overcoming procrastination is working out why we put things off. Once you know why you behave in a certain way, you can take steps to change. The issue of procrastination is less straightforward than it might seem. It isn't just about not getting on with things that we have to do, it is also associated with stress-related issues such as our personal and professional needs and motivation, and aspects of personality such as self-doubt, anxiety and self-esteem.

Fear of failure

This is a common cause of procrastination. It is a form of self-protection – if you don't do the task, you won't fail.

Scene 31: Pete's job application

Pete is bored and frustrated in his present position, where he has been for a long time. He would like to apply for another job, and gets as far as sending for the details of new positions. However, he never gets as far as completing an application. He tells himself he will do it 'later' when he is in the mood and can concentrate, but 'later' never comes. Really Pete fears that he will not get another job. If he never actually applies, he won't have to face the possibility of failure.

Fear of success
This might sound contradictory, but sometimes we do not want to complete a job because of the feelings which will arise when it is over. Perhaps completing a task successfully means that you will be free to move on to something else, and this makes you feel anxious. The sense of achievement when you successfully complete something can be mixed with regret at having to leave it behind. It might also be the case that succeeding in something does not fit your image of yourself; you might feel that you are not an achieving kind of person, and so back off from doing something that will cause you to reassess your self-valuation.

Dealing with others' reactions to your success could also be difficult. There might be changes in your personal or working relationships that you feel would be hard to handle.

Outcome not clearly visualized
If you do not have a clear picture of the end that you hope to achieve, your motivation to start or to keep going may be weak. Try to step into the future. Imagine as vividly as you can what it will be like when you have completed this job.

Satisfying control needs
Leaving things until the last minute could be your way of controlling other people. You may not be doing this consciously, but it is possible that you are trying to make others wait, to enhance the event of your arrival. You may wish to impose anxiety on others, causing them to feel tension about whether you will turn up, or whether you will complete a job or task. You might like the attention you gain from this behaviour.

Scene 32: Adam is always late

Adam never turns up on time for appointments or meetings. He says that this is not intentional. He claims that he wants to be punctual, and that he always thinks he is leaving enough time, but his behaviour does not support his claim. Adam puts off the moment of leaving. He makes just one more call, does just one more task. It is probable that Adam subconsciously enjoys the attention his late arrival and his reputation for tardiness attract – even if it is negative attention.

Meeting your stimulus needs
Another possible reason for always being late is that you enjoy the last-minute rush. Your pulse races as you try to beat the clock. You like the buzz of rushing to meetings and appointments, and are stimulated and energized by working all night to get something finished.

ACTIVITY 31: How you procrastinate

Choose three work tasks that you tend to put off. For each one, say why you put it off, and what you do instead.

Task	Why I put it off	What I do instead
1		
2		
3		

Ways of 'doing it now'

Remove your distractions

Look at what you do instead of the task you should be doing. One way of helping yourself to get on with it is to remove your escape or distraction! If you start to water the plants, move the plants to another room. If you feel the need to check how hot it is in Athens before you start work, remove the newspaper, turn off the television or radio. You might need to remove yourself and go to another space where your favourite distraction won't be to hand.

Small chunks

It is helpful to break the job down into small chunks, so that it does not look so daunting. You could write each chunk on a separate sheet of paper and focus just on the one bit you have chosen to do. This practice means that you do not have to set aside long periods of time – you could allocate just 15 minutes for some 'chunks'.

Commit yourself to small amounts of time

Decide to spend just five or ten minutes on whatever it is that you are putting off. Make sure that you get something done in that space of time. You can then decide whether you are going to commit another five or ten minutes.

Start anywhere

The habit of starting at the beginning and working through to the end is not always the most helpful. There will be some elements of a task that do not need to be done in sequence, and may be tackled at any point.

Go public

Telling someone else is a good way of making sure that you do something. Tell a suitable person, maybe a friend or your supervisor, what you intend to accomplish, and ask the person to ask you how you got on. You could also write down your goal and display it somewhere. Put stickers in all the places where you will see them regularly.

Do the worst first – or second

You could make the most unappealing task the first thing you do. This has the advantage of getting it out of the way so that you don't spend the whole day building up to doing it – or not doing it, as the case may be.

An alternative to this is to make the first task something that you enjoy, or at least something that is no problem to get out of the way. This can put you in a positive frame of mind, ready to tackle the object of your procrastination.

Finish in the middle

A piece of good advice is to finish a job that you have started. Unfortunately, this leaves chronic procrastinators with the huge task of getting going again. It can be helpful to stop a particular task at a point where it will be easy to pick it up again later to finish it off. This enables you to slide back into the task and gets the flow going.

Keep your stimulus level topped up

If you put things off because you enjoy the challenge of a last-minute rush, look for other, more positive ways of getting the stimulation that you need. Make specific plans to provide yourself with the amount of challenge and excitement that you need – a new project or assignment, learning something new which has an appropriate level of difficulty.

Build in a reward system

Make a list of all the treats which you would enjoy, and choose one as a reward for yourself every time you complete even the smallest task.

Dealing with interruptions

Being continually interrupted when you are trying to get on with something can lead to you feeling tense and tetchy, particularly when the cumulative effect of interruptions is that you are unable to complete your work. Commonly experienced interruptions are by people who want to chat, or want to ask you for something, such as a piece of information or help with their work. Try these techniques to cut short the interruption:

- Say, 'I'd love to hear all about your holiday/what happened last night later on when I will have time to listen properly.'
- Say, 'I must get this finished now, but I'll come over to you/ring you later.'
- If you see someone coming towards you, stand up.
- Finish a conversation by walking with the person towards the door or away from your workspace.
- Explore the possibility of a visual sign, such as a card in a particular colour or a certain object prominently displayed that people can use to indicate that they do not wish to be interrupted. You could choose something that is appropriate to your particular place of work.
- Set boundaries and deadlines straight away. Tell the person the amount of time that you have available.
- If you are frequently interrupted with questions and requests for help, you could prepare a checklist with some steps that people could take before coming to you. You could also review the way in which you delegate or give instructions. Are you making things clear?

ACTIVITY 32: Plan how to deal with interruptions

First of all, in a chart like the one below, track the interruptions that occur during a typical day. Fill in the chart every day for a week.

Nature of interruption   What the person wants Time it occurs   Length

1 _____

2 _____

3 _____

4 _____

5 _____

Once you are clear about the pattern of interruptions you can identify those that frequently occur and plan how you will handle them.

	Interruption	*What I will do/say*
1		
2		
3		
4		
5		

Email overload

The speed, immediacy and convenience of email mean that the volume of messages exchanged is continually growing to such an extent that many people spend several hours dealing with their mail, about a third of which is junk mail or irrelevant and unnecessary.

Allocate specific times

Decide that you will check your mail at certain, limited times of the day. Make this practice known. Not only will this help you to feel more in control, it will also stop others from expecting an instant reply.

Keep priorities in mind

If you begin the day by logging on to your mail it is likely that you will deal first with items that arise from it. You could be pushing your real priorities further down the line. Remind yourself that nothing should go to the top of your list just because it was communicated by email.

Limit what you send
Passing on jokes, gossip and other amusing items can be time-consuming for you and for the recipients. Ask yourself if the effect of what you are about to send is worth the investment of time and energy.

Use technology to manage technology
Developments in software manufacture mean that it is possible to control the email bombardment. Look out for functions such as the facility to reject email from certain senders, and the facility to recognize key words and arrange messages in order of importance.

ACTIVITY 33: Should I send this?

Think of some questions to ask yourself next time that you find yourself unable to resist sending a frivolous item, or something which you think is important or urgent. For example:

● Would this seem as funny/important if I had to work late or come in early in order to send it?
● Would I still send this if I had to use another form of communication?
● Would I still feel the same if I were in the middle of doing something very absorbing?

Don't copy in everybody
You could be building up stressful situations for yourself and for others if you copy in everyone you can think of when you send an email. This can have the effect of making you feel that you have dealt with the issue and passed on responsibility, when that may not in fact be the case. You are also adding to the pressure caused by the volume of messages.

Keep up interpersonal communication
Email may be used to forward documents, make arrangements to meet for a drink, set up meetings and so on. Sometimes these transactions take place between people who work in the same room.

You could try speaking face to face, or using the phone. Communication not only passes on information, it also strengthens relationships in the workplace and helps to reduce stress and tension.

Making better use of time

Delegate

Whenever you can, delegate tasks to suitable people. Effective delegation not only gets jobs done more quickly and efficiently, it also encourages and motivates people to develop skills. Bear in mind that delegation is not just a top-down activity: you can delegate tasks sideways and even upwards. For example, in a particular project your boss might have easier access than you to people and resources, and by making one or two calls on your behalf could save you lots of time.

Use 'dead' time

Many of us spend a lot of our time waiting – for traffic to clear, for the train to arrive, for an incoming call, to see someone. If you regard these pockets of time as wasteful, your levels of stress and frustration are likely to rise. Try planning to use this kind of 'dead' time in a constructive way:

- Always have a notebook of some kind so that you can do something constructive while you wait.
- Take the opportunity to practise breathing or relaxation exercises.
- Always have something useful or entertaining to read.
- If you enjoy puzzles or crosswords, keep one to hand to do unobtrusively.
- While travelling, listen to music or audio-books.

Add your own ideas:

_____

_____

_____

Make technology work for you

Many of us do not make full use of the technology at our disposal. Do you know how to use all the applications on your computer, or do you just use those that you are accustomed to? It is possible that spending a little time learning how to make better use of your machine will save you a lot of time in the long run, and enable you to deal with your workload more effectively. You could make things easier for yourself by becoming familiar with the multimedia technologies that might make your life easier. By using the facility of, for example, teleconferencing, you could make better use of your time and free yourself to plan long-term activities and focus on your major goals.

You might be in the habit of automatically printing out emails, or keeping hard copies of documents that you have on disk. Ask yourself if this is always necessary.

Learn to fix things

If your tension level rises as the photocopier jams or your printer will not work, you could save yourself time by learning how to put right some of the most common hitches. Invest a little time in finding out how to get things working again; you will not have the frustrating wait for someone to come and fix what has gone wrong.

De-clutter your workspace

You may lose lots of time and waste precious energy looking for papers and documents that have gone astray. It has been estimated that the time spent by the average office worker looking for lost documents amounts to eight days a year. Good organization can save you time and can also help you to withstand some of the daily pressures you encounter. Being organized means having some control over your environment as opposed to letting mess and clutter affect your feelings of energy. Some practices you could adopt include:

- scheduling regular clean-outs of equipment, files, computer disks;
- using books rather than odd pieces of paper for notes;
- keeping only essential items on your work area.

5

Strategies for a Stress-Proof Lifestyle

People who are resilient to pressure and who are less likely to suffer from the harmful effects of stress have certain characteristics. They accept that change is inevitable, and regard change rather than stability as an integral part of life. This kind of 'hardy' personality has developed attitudes and practices that manage the demands and challenges of pressure to create a confident, proactive approach to life.

Being in control

Take responsibility

People who manage stress effectively often display the belief that they are responsible for what goes on in their life. This does not mean that they feel the need to control events, but that they feel as if they have the power and ability to influence what happens, and they behave in accordance with this belief. They accept responsibility for their own emotions and actions rather than blaming external events or other people for things that go wrong.

Scene 33: Moira takes control

Rumours have been going around for some time, but Moira is still taken by surprise when it is announced that her department is being merged with another. This means that she will report to Carole, who she does not know very well, and also that she will work in a different area of the building. Moira feels very unsettled by these changes. She feels that her security is threatened, and that she is absolutely powerless to do anything about a situation which she dislikes. She wakes up at night with it on her mind, and is very tetchy with everyone at home. Moira notices that her co-worker Ethan seems to be much more comfortable with the situation than she is.

'I thought you'd be more upset,' she says. 'I'm really stressed out by all this, and it's their fault. Doesn't it get to you that they can impose these things on us and there's nothing we can do about it?'

During their conversation it emerges that Ethan has already spoken to Carole and feels better now that he's getting to know her. He also suggests that they go and have a look at the new area at lunch time so that he can discuss some changes he'd like to make to the layout.

Ethan's approach means that he is unlikely to suffer from stress-related ailments. He asks Carole why the decision was taken, and expresses his concern about the way that the merger has been handled. He does not harbour angry and resentful thoughts, or brood about unfairness, but chooses to reveal his feelings appropriately. He does not allow himself to feel like a passive victim. Unlike Moira, Ethan does not think that his emotional response to the situation is someone else's fault, and he looks for positive ways of taking control of the way he feels and of influencing the outcome of the new arrangements.

ACTIVITY 34: Taking control

Choose two situations that you find frustrating or stressful. Decide what you cannot alter, and what you can. Decide what positive attitude you will take to the things that you cannot do anything about.

Situation	What I can't control	What I can control	Positive thoughts
1			
2			

Have back-up

You will feel more in control of your life if you have a back-up plan to bring into play if your first preference falls through. To be effective, the back-up plan should be more than a vague idea; try to have your preparations ready so that you can put it into practice straight away. Not only will this course of action move you on to achieving your goal, it will also help you to deal with the feelings of frustration and negativity that you may experience when you receive a setback. Having a Plan B can make you feel happier and more positive in your present situation.

Scene 34: Cerys uses Plan B

Cerys wants to have more responsibility at work. She feels that she is ready to manage a major project, and is very excited when she is asked to apply for a particular project management job in her own company.

'I must be in with a good chance,' she says to her friend as they walk in the park at lunch time. 'After all, I've been approached about it.'

'I'm sure you're in a strong position,' her friend says. 'But I know that Mark has been asked to apply for it as well, and there may be one or two others.'

Cerys thinks about this. 'So if Mark or someone else got it, I would be working for them. I don't like that idea.'

Cerys is determined to put in a good application, and maintains her view of herself as the right person for the job, but she accepts that she may not be chosen. She plans what she will do should that happen. If she does not get this position she will immediately apply for something similar in another company. She researches the possibilities and updates her details to send out. If necessary, she will be ready to implement Plan B right away. In this way Cerys maintains her positive attitude. Knowing that she has another plan in place enhances her confidence and in fact helps her to prepare well for both her options.

ACTIVITY 35: Preparing a back-up plan

Think of something that you are hoping for at work – a successful job application or move, for example, or gaining a qualification. Decide on a plan to put into action should you not get the result you want. Break Plan B down into manageable steps so that you have something concrete to do immediately, as the example illustrates.

Goal: Pass my accountancy exam in July.

Plan B: Have ready the application form for posting off right away in case I need to retake.

Keep track of pressure

One way of maintaining control is to monitor your stress levels on a regular basis. Take stock of the kinds of pressure that you are experiencing and how you are dealing with them.

Harnessing pressure

Not only is pressure an inescapable part of life, it can actually be good for you. You can consolidate and build on the stress-proofing strategies we looked at in the previous chapter by learning how to harness pressure so that it becomes a positive force in your working life.

At some point in your life, you will probably have had the experience of doing something well when you were under pressure. You might have performed well in an exam, or in a sporting activity. You may have been pleased with the outcome when you were under pressure – for example, to complete a project in a certain time, or to give a presentation, or to conduct a tricky interview. In these situations it is highly likely that had you not been under pressure you would not have been so successful. The nature of the actual event you choose does not matter in itself. What matters is that you can tap into the sense of achievement and satisfaction that you felt at the time to give you a powerful reminder of the potentially energizing power of pressure. With practice, you can summon up this feeling to help you to become more positive when you begin to feel overwhelmed by the demands of a situation.

Scene 35: Pressure works for Omar

Omar is looking for another job, and gets very nervous about interviews. He has a few unsuccessful meetings, but learns from the experiences, and eventually has what he knows is a very good interview which results in a job offer.

100

Omar remembers what that last interview was like. He felt keyed-up and under pressure, with just the right amount of stimulation to help him to manage the interview so that he created a good impression. He could feel that he doing and saying the right things, and the little adrenaline buzz that he got from this spurred him on to maintain his good performance. When it was over, he felt exhilarated and confident about himself and his abilities.

Whenever Omar is in a testing situation and is not confident about his ability to cope, he re-creates the feelings that he had on that occasion. He relives the experience intensely, using his senses to bring it to life. He visualizes himself and the interviewer, and the details of the room they were in. He can feel the texture of his jacket, and smell the flowers that were on the desk. He hears the sound of the traffic outside, and the loud slam of a door down the corridor. Omar recalls what his body felt like, and the feeling of pleasure and achievement that flooded his mind.

By doing this, Omar replaces his fears about the present situation with a confident attitude. The vibrant memory of how he worked with pressure to bring about a good result makes him realize that he can do so again. He can now approach the situation with a more open frame of mind.

ACTIVITY 36: Make pressure work for you

Think of a time when being under pressure helped you to achieve something. Make your memory as vivid as you can, so that it is a kind of living snapshot. Practise tapping into this memory so that you can easily summon it up and relive it, and bring it to mind whenever you feel that you cannot cope with a situation. Make some notes to help you re-create the experience.

Event
What I can see
What I can hear
What I can feel or touch
What I can smell

Having commitment

One of the keys to a balanced, satisfying life is having an active interest in and involvement with a range of people and activities. People who display this characteristic show commitment to their way of life and to the values which inform their actions and choices. Developing this aspect of your life will increase your confidence and strengthen your resources to manage potentially stressful occasions and periods.

Commitment to a support system

Recognize the importance of having a support system, and plan how to keep it alive. See yourself as part of the system, and look for ways in which you can offer support as well as receive it. The sense of connection and purpose that comes from mutually supportive relationships enhances our sense of well-being and helps us to maintain our resilience to pressure.

ACTIVITY 37: Ways of giving support

1 What personal characteristics can you offer? Tick any of the following that apply to you.

honesty
empathy
respect for others
thoughtful
able to analyse
sense of humour
willing to listen
willing to express feelings and thoughts
non-judgemental

Add your own ideas:

_____

_____

_____

2 What skills do you have to offer? Tick any of the following that apply to you.

able to guide
able to advise
can offer practical help
sharing information
can bring about changes
an active and effective listener
can give feedback

Add your own ideas:

_____

_____

_____

_____

Creating a support system

Try to create a support system that meets a range of needs. Cultivate and nourish a network of people who sustain you in different ways. At times you may need to talk about emotional issues, at other times you might want to discuss work-related issues with someone in the same line of work as you. Sometimes we want to be with people who are good fun and make us laugh. Make sure that you have in your support system people who themselves have a positive outlook on life.

ACTIVITY 38: Your network of support

Here are some examples of types of people you could include. Think of a person for each category (some individuals may fit several descriptions).

Description	*Person*
Someone who:	
Makes me laugh	
Helps me talk through problems	
Gives good advice	
Makes me feel good about myself	
Challenges me	
Enjoys the same leisure activities	
Makes me think	
Is a source of helpful information	
I can confide in	
Offers practical help	
Helps me to relax	
I can discuss work problems with	
Is nothing to do with my work	

ACTIVITY 39: Circles of support

In the inner circle, write the names of the people who are closest to you. Move out through the outer rings, writing in names according to their significance in your life. Include distant relationships, people who have helped you in the past, people who you do not know well but who have given you verbal or non-verbal encouragement, or have just made you feel good about yourself.

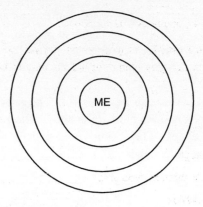

Figure 6 Circles of support

Commitment to a purpose

Having a sense of purpose and direction increases our resilience to pressure by giving focus and meaning to our lives. The goals and values that you identified earlier are what give shape to what you do. Maintain your concentration on living a life that displays your commitment to your value system.

ACTIVITY 40: Your personal mission statement

Write a statement that sets out your personal vision of life. This statement should include your basic purpose in work and in life, your values and goals. Make this statement of purpose your touchstone and reference point for all your actions and decisions.

Embracing challenge

People who see opportunities instead of threats and who can turn all situations into possibilities for personal growth and development are able to thrive in the face of change.

Life changes

Coping with change can be stressful. The work of psychologists Thomas Holmes and Richard Rahe shows the relationship between stress and life events. They published a scale of 43 activities and the levels of stress associated with them.

ACTIVITY 41: Stressful events

How much stress would you associate with each of the following events? Put them in order, starting with the most stressful.

(a) losing your job; (b) getting married; (c) getting divorced; (d) a change in your responsibilities at work; (e) dealing with major changes at work; (f) your son or daughter leaving home; (g) separation from your partner; (h) dealing with Christmas; (i) death of your partner.

Check your answers at the end of the chapter, p. 120.

Anticipating change

You will have noticed that even sought-after and pleasurable changes can trigger some degree of stress. Be prepared for the impact of a major career or life event to hit you about six months after the event – you might find yourself suffering some of the symptoms we looked at in Chapter 2. Also look out for periods when you experience a series of changes in a short time. The cumulative effect of a number of even minor events can be severe. When you know that a significant event is going to take place, you can put into place some strategies to help you to remain calm.

The benefits of change

Although you might go through a tough time as you adapt to a new situation, if you manage the transition period effectively and receive appropriate understanding and support, once you are through it you are likely to experience a burst of positive energy. This is the point at which many individuals display innovative and adaptive skills, and perform at their highest level.

Living with change

If you accept change as normal and something to be welcomed rather than feared, you will be able to thrive in times of pressure. Of course, not every type of change is welcome or positive, but it is easier to handle if you accept it and look for what can grow out of it. If you resist the very idea of things changing, you may be categorized as backward-looking or stuck in a rut.

Some of the major changes that have taken place in our working lives include shifts in culture and expectations. Stability has given way to change, and things that were once predictable, such as the nature of your job, how you did it and for how long, are now uncertain. Loyalty was once a valued characteristic; now we are judged by performance targets. Rather than progress along one career path, we are now likely to have several careers in our working lives, and to engage in lifelong learning to develop new skills and attitudes.

If you can see change such as this as challenging rather than daunting, and can have a mental attitude that combines a positive approach with a realistic appraisal of your coping strategies and how you can strengthen them, you may find change to be energizing and stimulating.

Work/life balance

You will create a healthy balance between your work and all the other aspects of your life by looking at your life as a whole, and establishing criteria for your own definition of success in each area. The amount of energy and attention that you give to each element will vary according to individual and changing circumstances, but

STRATEGIES FOR A STRESS-PROOF LIFESTYLE

your life can slip too far out of balance if you consistently neglect certain aspects and pour all your energies into one or two main areas. If you maintain a balanced lifestyle and a sense of perspective the pressures and strains of everyday life become manageable.

How balanced are you?

Think of the main areas of your life:

- *Work:* This includes your job, how you work, feelings about work, your motivation, future plans.
- *Family and personal relationships:* This area contains your central relationships, the people who are sources of support and comfort.
- *Social activity:* This encompasses elements of your life such as going out, spending time with others, leisure activities.
- *Financial:* Included here are aspects such as debts, savings, planning for the future, the part that money plays in your life.
- *Community life:* This refers to a wider focus and an involvement with society.
- *Inner/spiritual life:* This refers to your spiritual well-being, and includes aspects such as your sense of inner purpose and your regard for things beyond the material and the worldly.
- *Health:* Caring for your physical and mental health, covering areas such as diet and exercise.
- *Your own ideas:* Add any aspects of your life that are not covered by these categories.

_____

_____

ACTIVITY 42: Life circle

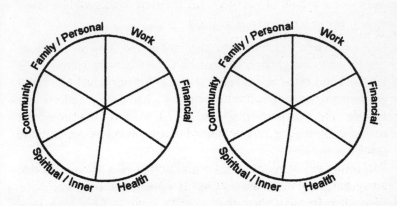

Figure 7 Life circles

The segments in the circles represent aspects of your life.

Circle 1: In each segment write a number between 1 and 10 which represents the amount of time and energy you devote to each area.

Circle 2: In each segment write a number between 1 and 10 which represents the amount of time and energy you would like to devote to each area.

Balance of roles

We all have a number of roles in our lives. In different contexts you might be a parent, a daughter or son, a friend, a colleague, a boss, a sister, a brother, a team-mate, a church member and so on. We define ourselves in different ways according to the situation. If you define yourself exclusively by your work role, putting all your time and energy into your career, then your relationships and involvement with family, friends and community are likely to suffer.

You will reduce the likelihood of stress if you maintain a balance between your roles, and if you aim to develop and foster those which are most important to you.

Scene 36: Heidi invests too much in one role

Heidi's job as a management consultant in a top city firm requires her to work long hours, sometimes until the early hours of the morning and often at weekends as well. All her time and energy go into proving herself at work, and her salary reflects her success. Heidi expects that she will be chosen to head up the forthcoming project in New York. However, a co-worker is given this responsibility.

Heidi is devastated. She feels totally flattened, and thinks that everyone at work is talking about her failure. She feels worthless, as if all that she is and all that she has worked for have been wiped out.

Heidi has invested too much of herself in one role. Her self-esteem is dependent on how she sees herself and is seen in a work context. Her commitment to work means that she has neglected other areas of her life and so has no ready source from which she can rebuild her feeling of self-worth and identity.

ACTIVITY 43: Your key roles

Which are the most important roles that you have in your work and in your private life? For each one, decide what you want to achieve and how you will achieve it.

Role	What I want to achieve	How I will achieve it
1		
2		

3 _____

4 _____

5 _____

6 _____

_____

Setting personal goals

_____

ACTIVITY 44: Whole life goals

Write down three goals for each of these aspects of your life. Remember to express your goals in concrete, positive terms, and to give them a deadline.

What I want to achieve   By when   How I will know I am succeeding

Personal and family relationships

1 _____

2 _____

3 _____

Social life

1 _____

2 _____

3 _____

STRATEGIES FOR A STRESS-PROOF LIFESTYLE

Financial

1 _____

2 _____

3 _____

Health

1 _____

2 _____

3 _____

Religious, spiritual or inner life

1 _____

2 _____

3 _____

Community involvement

1 _____

2 _____

3 _____

Your own ideas

_____

_____

Different ways of working

You may be able to create or restore some balance in your life by changing your hours and conditions of work.

Scene 37: Lena arranges a job-share

Lena has returned to full-time work after the birth of her second child, but is finding it very hard to meet the demands of her job and the needs of her two young children. She needs to work and likes her job, and does not want to give up everything she has achieved at work.

'Juggling it all is so hard,' she tells a friend. 'It's making me so tired that I don't know how long I'll go on doing a good job anyway!'

'What about going part-time?' her friend suggests.

Lena grimaces. 'I couldn't go part-time and keep my clients. But fewer hours would be great.'

Lena thinks about other options, and comes up with the idea of a job-share. One of her work colleagues, Steph, is in a similar situation, finding it tough to manage full-time work and home commitments. Lena thinks that she and Steph could successfully job-share. They get on well together and work the same way.

Steph is delighted with the proposal, and they discuss ways of splitting the week between them. They decide to ask for three days each, with one day as a cross-over for planning and liaising. When they get the go-ahead for the plan, Lena and Steph spend some time sorting out the precise details of the job breakdown, so that each of them is very sure about her responsibilities. They feel that this ground work will get their job-share off to a really good start.

Alternative working arrangements

There is a range of alternative ways of working which you could consider. Decide what you want to achieve through making a change, and how the change that you propose could make your life less stressful.

- *Job-sharing:* This is the term used when two people split one job. The sharers divide pay, holiday and other benefits.
- *Part-time working:* This is defined as fewer than 30 hours a week.
- *Flexitime hours:* In this system, you have some leeway about the hours that you work. You do a fixed number of hours in the week, but can choose, for example, when you start and finish (usually within certain stated limits).
- *Compressed weeks:* This is a system in which you work the same number of hours in a week, but they are compressed into fewer days. So you work longer days, but you do not work every day. You might work a nine-day fortnight, for example, or work four ten-hour days.
- *Staggered hours:* This system is often used to allow employers to cover long hours. All employees can start and finish at different times.
- *Teleworking:* This involves working from home for all or most of the time. You will use a telephone and computer to keep in touch with work.
- *V-time:* This kind of working involves you taking a voluntary reduction in pay and hours, usually for a fixed period of time.
- *Term-time working:* As the name suggests, this is where you work paid hours during school terms only, taking the thirteen weeks or so school holiday periods as unpaid leave.

ACTIVITY 45: Different ways of working

What do you think would be the best option or options for each of the following?

- someone who wants one day off every week;
- someone who finds commuting very stressful;
- someone who wants to spend more time with his children but who cannot afford to cut his hours;
- someone who wants a break from work until the children go to secondary school;
- someone who prefers to work late and start early;
- someone who wants to go on a round-the-world trip.

If you are considering a change in your working pattern, there are a number of factors to bear in mind. Make sure that the proposed change is the right one to give you the balance that you require, and that it supports your goals and values. For example, if you are thinking of working from home to ease the pressure of commuting, you may need to weigh the strain of a difficult journey to work against the stimulus of working with other people.

Personal optimism

People who are generally optimistic are more able to deal positively with pressure than those whose outlook is negative and pessimistic. Most of us are a mixture of both attitudes, and exhibit different traits in different circumstances – it is unrealistic to expect to be positive all the time, and it is harmful to your mental and physical well-being to assume that you can never be positive. You can develop an optimistic attitude by applying strategies that help to keep negative factors at bay. This requires you to develop ways of bringing the positive into focus, making it stronger than any negative thoughts that surface.

Language matters

The words and phrases that we habitually use reflect our mood and attitude, and can also influence the way that we feel. It is difficult to feel positive in the midst of constant moaning and griping, our own or other people's – you can actually begin a conversation feeling okay, only to find that you have been talked into or have talked yourself into a negative mood. Sometimes conversations are of necessity downbeat and focus on negative factors, but there is no reason why casual encounters and brief conversations should always draw attention to what is wrong. Criticizing your boss or colleagues, talking about illness, describing a terrible holiday or night out all have their place in the currency of conversation, but if such topics dominate every encounter and exclude any positive exchanges it can be hard to maintain a positive working environment.

The language you use influences the way that you feel about

yourself and the way that others react to you. Using positive language can help you to achieve your work goals. It will lead other people to respond to you in a co-operative and positive way, because the words that you use connect with their own store of positive references and memories. It also means that you will feel more optimistic and confident.

Scene 38: Affirmative speech

On separate occasions, Liane and Jane talk to their manager about difficulties they are having in processing orders.

Liane says, 'The problem is dealing with head office. You might as well talk to a brick wall. It's just such hard work trying to get through to them!'

Jane says, 'As I see it, the best way to solve this is to find a method of communicating with head office.'

Liane's language focuses on problems and difficulties, and expresses frustration and annoyance. The words that Jane uses reflect a positive attitude, which generates a feeling of energy and possibility, both in herself and in the person with whom she is speaking.

Talking positively

You could try to make even your casual conversation positive and upbeat. This does not mean that you have to pretend that everything is fine, but if you are, for example, describing a disastrous occasion, present it humorously, or end the account on a positive note, even if it is just a resolution never to be in that position again. Monitor the kind of language that you use – if you describe everything as 'awful' or 'terrible' or 'disastrous' your stress levels are likely to increase as you lose your sense of proportion and talk yourself into seeing things as much worse than they really are.

Of course, there are times when you want to discuss a problem or talk about something upsetting. Choose someone from your support network, a friend or colleague, who will listen actively and receptively.

Words to use		*Words to avoid*
great	wonderful	nightmare
terrific	delighted	trouble
challenge	giggle	hard
exciting	fantastic	difficult
tremendous	invigorating	terrible
opportunity	superb	awful
laugh	peaceful	disaster
happy	stimulating	problem
amazing		hassle
pleased		frustration

ACTIVITY 46: The words that you use

Award yourself a point every time you use a word which has a positive feel. You could keep a running total in a notebook, and treat yourself when you reach a certain target. (See p. 130 for suggestions.)

The power of praise

Praise is a great motivator. Giving and receiving praise for something done well increases our confidence and gives a huge boost to our sense of well-being. The positive psychological effect of praise can help to keep at bay some of the harmful effects of working under pressure. In spite of this, praising others is something that is rarely done. Some reasons for not giving praise include fear that it will seem patronizing or insincere, or that it will be embarrassing for the giver and the receiver. However, you can learn to offer and accept praise in a way that is open and direct, and helps to create in your place of work a positive culture in which people's contribution is valued.

How to give praise

Identify precisely what it is that you admire or appreciate

A general comment such as 'Well done' or 'You did a good job there' is valuable, but not as powerful as recognition of something specific. For example, if you wish to commend someone who has made a good presentation, or handled a difficult client or customer well, you could say, 'That was a very good presentation. I liked the way you made the figures so clear,' or 'You answered those tricky questions very confidently.'

Keep it brief, direct and positive

You will detract from the impact of what you say if you say too much, or if you add anything negative.

Keep the spotlight on the other person

This is the other person's moment. Do not turn the attention away, by referring to yourself, for example. A comment such as 'I couldn't have done it so well' takes the spotlight off the other person, and rather invites some reciprocal praise – which is not the point of the communication.

Give praise whenever you think it is deserved

Some people think that it is only appropriate for a senior to praise someone junior to them. This is far from the case – if someone working alongside you does something that you think is really good, tell them so. If your boss has done something praiseworthy, don't feel that it is inappropriate to express your admiration. After all, even those in senior positions can get anxious about presentations or meetings or negotiations. It is always good to be told when something goes well, particularly if it is something that has caused a lot of thought, worry or preparation.

By giving credit where credit is due in these thoughtful, sincere ways, you can help to shape the culture of your workplace, making it the kind of place where praise is the norm – a positive antidote to stress.

ACTIVITY 47: Giving credit where credit is due

Think of three occasions when you have made a complimentary remark about what someone has done – but you said it to a third party, not to the person involved! Decide what you could have said to the person involved.

What I said to a third party	*What I could have said to the person*
That promotional display that Lou organized is really effective.	Lou, that display looks great! I love the photomontage in particular.

1 _____

2 _____

3 _____

How to receive praise

Accept the praise
Maintain eye contact with the speaker, smile and say thank you. A comment like 'I appreciate you telling me' shows that you acknowledge the positive nature of the action. If the person speaking is, for example, an expert in the area of work he or she is commenting on, or someone who has contributed to your success, you might reflect your awareness of this by saying something like 'I appreciate your response in particular because . . .'

Do not disagree with or qualify what has been said
If you say something like 'Oh, it wasn't really that good,' or 'It would have been better if . . .' you are doing the equivalent of throwing back a present that someone has given you.

Do not feel obliged to say something in return
Treat the feedback as a positive comment on your professional capacity, and do not behave as if you think that the speaker is fishing for a reciprocal compliment!

If necessary, ask for more information

If someone has been vaguely complimentary about something you have done, you could ask them to be more specific. You might be concerned that this will sound as if you are asking for more praise to be heaped on you, but in fact this behaviour is helpful and professional. So if someone says, 'You did a good job at the function last night,' you might say, 'Thanks. I appreciate that. What did you think worked well?' This helps the person to be more precise, and perhaps say, 'You kept very calm when there was a rush, and I noticed how pleasantly you dealt with the complaint about the wine.'

By building positive factors into your working environment and your personal focus, you will increase your immunity to the harmful effects of stress.

Answers to Stressful events, p. 106
Order: i, c, g, b, a, e, d and f, h.

The numbers show the relative degree of stress associated with each event:

(a) 47
(b) 50
(c) 73
(d) 29
(e) 39
(f) 29
(g) 65
(h) 12
(i) 100.

6

Self-Care for Your Body and Mind

Looking after yourself is an essential part of managing the pressures of your life at work and outside work.

The art of relaxation

You can control your response to stress and bring your body and mind into a state of calm through deliberate relaxation. Relaxation is a skill that you can learn and that you need to practise, but once you have learnt some methods that work for you, you will be able to use them to lower your stress levels and to feel in control. By practising positive relaxation you get rid of the tension from your muscles and clear your mind of anxiety. Build relaxation into your life by learning some techniques that you can use while you are at work, and consolidate them with some structured relaxation sessions in your own time.

Instant checks for physical tension

Sometimes we do not realize that we are physically tense. Throughout the day, check to see if you are doing any of the following:

- clenching your toes;
- tensing the muscles of your calf and backside;
- tapping your toes;
- hunching your shoulders;
- clenching your stomach muscles;
- biting your nails;
- tapping or swinging your foot.

Your own examples:

_____

_____

Breathing

Breathing properly is the key to feeling relaxed. When we feel under pressure we breathe quickly and from high in the chest, which causes too much carbon dioxide to be released into the bloodstream, slows down the circulation of oxygen and has a number of unpleasant effects such as faintness, numbness and tingling in the nerves. It is better for you to breathe slowly and gently from the diaphragm. This kind of breathing makes sure that enough oxygen flows around your body without too much carbon dioxide being expelled. It helps you to relax and reduces tension and anxiety.

Breathing exercises you can do at work

Here is an exercise that you can do in five minutes in your workplace, travelling to work or sitting in a traffic jam. Sit up straight, to allow your diaphragm to work properly, and take a deep breath, counting up to five as you breathe in through your nose. You will probably feel your chest rising. Breathe out slowly, keeping your chest in the up position and feeling your stomach fall. Breathe in and out again, feeling your stomach muscles rise and fall. Make sure you expel all the air from your lungs. You know that you are breathing properly when your chest does not move and your stomach does.

You can do this kind of slow rhythmic breathing several times during the day. Bring it into play in situations when you are put under pressure. On occasions when you want to take a few seconds before you respond to a comment or a request, start to breathe in this way as you consider your response, and you will feel calm and in control.

Deep breathing exercises

Do this exercise at home to help you to wind down after work.

Lie on the floor, close your eyes and begin to breathe in through your nose. Feel your ribcage and your chest expanding. Breathe out slowly through your nose, making this breath last twice as long as your in-breath. Repeat this a few times.

As you breathe in, raise your arms at the same pace until the backs of your hands touch the floor. Lower your arms as you breathe out. This helps you to breathe efficiently from your diaphragm.

Relaxing your muscles and mind

Muscle relaxing exercises that you can do at work

Sitting at a desk or doing a lot of driving are just two activities that can cause tension in your shoulders and neck. Loosen up these muscles by keeping your arms loose and relaxed, dropping your shoulders as far as you can, then rolling them forward in a circular movement, bringing them high up towards your neck. Spend a minute or two on these circular movements. Then repeat the process, rotating your shoulders in a backward movement.

Muscle relaxing exercises that you can do at home

You can also employ systematic relaxation of all your muscle groups, an exercise which can very quickly induce a state of calm. Choose a quiet place where you can sit or lie down very comfortably. Concentrate on each part of your body in turn, starting with your head. For each section of your body, tense the muscles, hold them tense for a few seconds, then relax them. Breathe out fully as you feel the tension disappear. Empty your mind of all thoughts – just concentrate on what you are feeling in the section that you are exercising.

You can make the experience more intense by combining it with visualization. Bring to mind a picture that you find soothing – it may be a place that brings to mind peace and tranquillity, or an image which you associate with calm. You can also choose a word or phrase such as 'calm' or 'easy now' to accompany the act of breathing out and the release of tension.

When you are used to this activity, you could use it at work when you need to de-stress quickly. Find a quiet spot and go through the exercise. Get into the habit of activating your relaxation response instead of your stress response.

Getting rid of a tension headache

You can do this sitting or standing, preferably near a source of fresh air. Drop your chin down to your chest then up again. With your fingertips, massage the back of your neck. Then knead your neck in circular movements several times.

Systematic relaxation of the muscles in your face, head and

shoulders will also help. Hunger or dehydration might be contributing to your headache – have something suitable to eat and drink. If headaches persist, consult your doctor.

Meditation

Many people find that learning to meditate helps them to become relaxed. There are various forms of meditation.

A practice such as transcendental meditation works on the mind to relax the body. By quietening down and settling your mind, you bring your body and mind into a state of profound restfulness, empty of thoughts and concerns. This particular type of meditation uses a mantra, a word or phrase of your own choice or creation which is chanted, and the technique does need to be taught, but once you have learnt it you do not need to keep seeing an instructor.

Buddhist meditation uses a technique called 'mindfulness' in which you experience and value the present moment. This practice can help you to keep calm in times of pressure. When you are feeling rushed at work, stop and sink into what is going on around you. Let your senses focus intensely only on the present and what you experience in the here-and-now – the effect of light, of sound, of what you can touch and see, what your body feels like and how it responds. This stops anxious thoughts crowding into your mind.

If you think that meditation is for you, you could make it one of your priorities to find out details of courses and lessons that you could attend.

Yoga

Yoga works on the body to relax the mind. It combines breathing and relaxation techniques with meditation and stretching exercises, in which you use different postures to bring about a state of mental and physical well-being and balance. Again, you need to learn the techniques from an experienced and qualified teacher. Yoga can be a vigorous physical exercise, so think carefully if you have any muscular conditions, such as a weak back, which should be taken into account.

If you are receiving treatment for any condition, or if you know there is cause for concern about certain areas of your health, do check with your doctor before you start a new form of exercise.

Autogenic training

This is a system of relaxation in which you control your physical tension through a series of mental exercises. You concentrate on six different areas of focus, such as heaviness in your arms and legs, warmth, calm breathing, your heartbeat. Once you have learnt how to do the exercises, you should do them several times a day to bring about a state of calm and relaxation.

A stress-proof way of eating

What you eat affects the way that you feel and can help you to cope with pressure. The right kind of food builds up your energy levels and strengthens your immune system, as well as improving your circulation and maintaining your blood sugar at a steady level. Food not only fuels your body and mind, but can also be a source of comfort, pleasure and relaxation.

In a busy working day it is all too easy to overlook these factors. If you are very caught up in what you are doing, you might forget to eat, maybe until you are reminded by the onset of a headache or migraine. You may choose unhealthy food, because it is easily available or because you want a quick sugar fix, or because you want to feel comforted by what you eat. Try to look on food as your ally in the fight against stress, and build it into your working day, making healthy and helpful choices about your diet.

What to eat when

Eating a little and often is a good way to keep your blood sugar levels steady and to maintain your energy and concentration. You really should begin with breakfast, a meal which is often skipped because of lack of time. If you have time to eat at home choose something like cereal, eggs, baked beans, wholemeal toast. Fibre-rich food such as porridge, muesli or granary bread is a good choice because it releases energy slowly so you feel full up for longer and don't get an energy dip. If you grab something on the way to work, try to steer clear of sugary pastries – sugar is released very quickly into the bloodstream and gives you a short-term boost, but your energy will fade. Pick up some fruit salad or yoghurt instead. At lunch time go for something with protein rather than a high-carbohydrate meal based on bread, pasta or potatoes which may make you sleepy. If you make your own lunch-time sandwich, or have one made up in a shop or café, get a filling which contains protein and in which the filling is thicker than the bread. You will get protein from meat, fish, chicken, beans and pulses and soya-based food. Do choose carbohydrates for small snacks, however, because they are absorbed slowly into your body and give you a steady supply of energy. The best type of carbohydrate is unrefined, which comes in wholegrain bread, nuts, fruit and vegetables.

In the evening, a meal based on pasta or rice will help you to wind down and feel sleepy.

Try to build in the recommended five servings of fruit and vegetables a day. Fruit is particularly good for anyone who works on a VDU all day, because it contains antioxidants which protect the eyes. Get into the habit of adding tomato, cucumber or lettuce to sandwiches, and taking an apple or banana to work with you.

Making choices about what you eat

If you buy lunch from a food shop, supermarket or canteen you should find it possible to choose something to eat that is healthy, tasty and will keep you going through an afternoon's work. Try to vary what you eat, and experiment with items that are different from your usual choice. You can eat more healthily by making slight adjustments to your diet.

Instead of	Try
crisps	dried fruit
salted nuts	unsalted nuts
sugary biscuits	flapjacks, oat biscuits
mayonnaise	mustard
ordinary chocolate	70 per cent cocoa solids chocolate
refined sugar	honey, fresh fruit
cream	yoghurt
white rice	brown rice
fried	boiled, steamed, baked, grilled

Making choices about what you drink

Be careful with your alcohol consumption. Keep within the recommended unit guidelines, and don't save up your 'allowance' for one session of binge drinking. (You can check guidelines for drinking on one of the government/national health service websites.) If you are going for a drink after work, eat something first.

Be careful with your caffeine consumption. Caffeine is a stimulant which actually puts you into stress response mode by making your heart beat faster and increasing your blood pressure. Caffeine is found not only in coffee, but in tea and soft drinks. If you enjoy tea or coffee, save your caffeine 'allowance' for a few good cups a day which you can look forward to.

Drink lots of water. If there is a water cooler in your workplace, make full use of it. Keep a bottle of water with you as you work. When you feel thirsty or feel that you would like a drink, get in the habit of choosing water instead of a can or bottle of something sugary and caffeinated.

Physical exercise

Regular exercise keeps you physically fit and mentally alert. Physical activity protects you from the harmful effects of stress in numerous ways. It gives you an outlet for built-up energy, it helps your heart and lungs to work effectively, lowers your blood pressure and strengthens your immune system. Exercise also makes you feel good. It produces beta-endorphins, natural chemicals which raise your spirits and make you feel happy, and other mood-affecting chemicals such as seratonin and dopamine are generated in your brain when you exercise. Physical exercise also has a good effect on your mind. Aerobic exercise increases the oxygen supply to the brain, making you mentally more alert and effective.

It can be difficult to fit in regular exercise. Many of us lead fairly sedentary lives and can go for long periods of time without any significant physical activity. You may feel that you do not have the time for a regular commitment. However, the fact is that you will not manage stress effectively without adequate physical exercise.

You could consider two broad approaches to the question of how to fit in exercise:

1 Build some exercise into your working day.
2 Plan physical activities which will help you to achieve your work/
   life balance goals.

Built-in exercise

You could get off the bus or train a stop earlier and walk the
remainder of your journey.
You could park at a suitable distance from your workplace.
Try using stairs instead of lifts and escalators.
Walking for 20 minutes three times a week can benefit your heart,
lungs and circulation – you could take a walk at lunch time on three
days of the week. Not only will you benefit from the physical
activity, the break from work will do you good. If you can find a
pleasant environment such as a park or riverside you will also boost
your inner well-being. If you dislike the idea of walking for
walking's sake, plan an end goal. Think of somewhere a suitable
distance away where you can buy a newspaper or magazine, for
example.

Exercise and your goals

Use physical activity as a way of maintaining balance in your life.
Walking, swimming, jogging, cycling, dancing, aerobic exercise
classes and gym sessions are the kind of exercise which will give
you maximum physical benefit and which could at the same time
meet some of your other needs.
   You can maintain and develop friendships and nurture your
support group by exercising with a friend or group of friends. When
you have a mutual commitment to a planned activity you are less
likely to find excuses not to turn up, and you help to keep each other
motivated.
   Make exercise a social event. Dancing is great exercise, and you
benefit from the music and the company as well. If you go to an
exercise class, arrange to go on to something afterwards, or to share
a meal.
   Exercise can provide you with pleasure and enjoyment. Don't do
anything you dislike because you think it will be good for you –
there will be something that you enjoy.
   Combine exercise with self-development. You could learn a

language, or read or listen to books or music while you use a machine at the gym.

ACTIVITY 48: Physical activity

Decide how you will increase your resistance to stress through physical exercise.

What I will do	Physical benefits	Other benefits	Start date

Renew and recharge

Find ways of introducing or reintroducing fun and pleasure into your life.

Have a good laugh

Laughing relieves stress. Humour helps you to see things in perspective. Identify from your network people whose sense of humour you enjoy and share, and plan to spend time with them. Go to see films and shows that make you laugh, cut out and display cartoons that you find funny.

Have a good cry

Becoming emotionally involved in a play or a book or a film and releasing your tension through tears is cathartic and healthy. Don't feel embarrassed – let yourself go.

129

Have a good talk

Communication can give you a powerful boost. Make time for conversation with friends. Share experiences and thoughts generously. As you know, it is helpful and healthy to talk about your problems with a suitable person.

Make time for activities that you enjoy

Many of us harbour thoughts about things that we would like to do, if only we had the time . . . ! Make time for what you enjoy. Put activities that you find fulfilling at the top of your priority list. Let ideas emerge from the back of your mind. There might be a book you have always wanted to read, a place you would like to visit, something you would like to learn, people you would like to spend more time with.

If you feel that you have lost the knack of enjoying yourself, think back to when you were a child. What kind of activity did you enjoy? Think of how you could incorporate elements of those activities into your adult life.

Give yourself treats

Build in your own system of treats and rewards. They need not be extravagant or expensive – make a list of ways in which you like to pamper and indulge yourself and take pleasure in regularly choosing something from your list.

7

The Stress-Proof Organization

Why you should take stress seriously

Whether you are an employer or an employee, there are steps that you can take to minimize the harmful effects of stress at work. There are two main benefits for employers of taking an involved, proactive approach to stress in your workplace. First, you will avoid the threat of possible legal action against your organization, and second, and in the long run more importantly, you will improve the quality of life for your work force, which will result in greater motivation and commitment. Employees who experience work-related stress can also take action to protect themselves.

Your legal obligations as an employer

Companies and institutions are obliged to become aware of the sources of stress at work, and to take reasonable steps to protect individuals from harm. There are several pieces of legislation which are concerned with employers' responsibilities and liabilities:

- the Health and Safety at Work Act (1974);
- the Employment Protection Act (1978);
- the Sex Discrimination Act (1975);
- the Race Relations Act (1976);
- the Disability Discrimination Act (1995).

It is important to know what the law says about the responsibility of organizations with reference to stress at work. The main point to bear in mind is that it is an employer's duty to deal with a situation once an employee has made the employer aware of the symptoms of stress. If it is clear that some harm will ensue as a result of the stress that someone is experiencing, then you must take steps to deal with the problem. If an employee can prove that your negligence or failure of duty has contributed to the stress-related illness, and that the risk of illness was foreseeable, he or she may have grounds for a complaint against you. Once you have identified that someone is suffering from stress, you have scope to decide how you tackle it, depending on the size of your organization and the resources at your disposal – for example, there is no obligation to make rearrangements for the sake of one person, and there is no need for you to take a course of action if it would have an unwelcome effect on other employees.

What an employee should do

If you are suffering stress-related symptoms, it is your responsibility to make your employer aware of this. You should:

1 make a written complaint when you first suffer the symptoms of stress;
2 keep a record of every subsequent stress-causing incident or situation.

Remember that your employer will not be aware of what is going on inside your head, nor of pressures on you outside the workplace. Unless your employer knows that you suffer from a particular problem that may affect your work performance, it will be assumed that you are capable of doing your job. It is in your interests to bring stressful situations to the attention of your employer – do not suffer in silence if you have an unacceptably high workload, or are given unrealistic deadlines. (Chapter 4 gives you some ideas about how to communicate such matters.)

Scene 39: Kevin does not reveal that he is under stress

Kevin covers a large geographical area in his job as a sales representative. He finds it very difficult to cope with the workload this imposes.

'Say something to them at work,' his wife urges. 'Perhaps they could split up the areas a bit more.'

'I don't want to do that. They'll think I can't cope.'

The strain becomes too much for Kevin and he becomes anxious and depressed, having to take a period of time off work. The company promises to reduce the size of his area. However, when Kevin returns to work, this has not been done, and he is faced with the same situation as before. He begins to experience the same symptoms as before, and becomes ill again.

In this case, Kevin's employer could be liable for damages with respect to the second period of illness, which was foreseeable. The company had not kept its promise to change the conditions of work which led to Kevin's illness. The employers would not be liable for Kevin's first illness, as he had not given any indication that he was under stress.

However, it is unhelpful and unhealthy to see the issue entirely in terms of culpability and liability. A more productive approach for everyone is to address the issue before it becomes a matter of confrontation. It is in everyone's interests to work together to prevent and fight occupational stress.

What managers can do to minimize stress

It makes sense for you to tackle the sources of stress at your place of work and to do as much as you can to prevent stress from becoming an issue. There are things that you can do to deal with situations which arise, such as helping individuals who suffer stress-related illnesses to recover and to resume work, but a better long-term plan would be to put into place strategies and practices which help to prevent the harmful effects of stress by eliminating or reducing sources of stress. First of all, identify the stressors in your workplace, then decide what specific changes you can make to remove or reduce their harmful impact.

You could begin by considering two main categories: the physical conditions in which people work, and the management style of the company – your own personal style or that of line managers, department heads, supervisors, or anyone who has responsibility for people at work. For each category, you could draw up a list of questions focusing on areas of potential stress. There are several ways of getting answers to the questions:

- ask your team to respond to an anonymous questionnaire;
- ask individuals privately for their response to particular questions;
- answer them yourself, from self-knowledge and knowledge and observation;
- use them as the basis for discussion with the team or with individuals.

You could try a combination of the above suggestions, as you think appropriate. The more you talk and listen, the greater knowledge and understanding you will gain about how people are feeling.

Your management style

Good management will prevent stress-related problems. Supportive management activities include:

- matching people to the job;
- making sure that demands are at the right level for the individual;
- talking to people about their role;
- making sure that everyone has clearly defined responsibilities;
- making sure that people know what is expected of them;
- having clear systems and policies to deal with difficult situations;
- valuing and respecting individuals;
- managing change sensitively;
- encouraging a healthy work/life balance;
- encouraging participation and discussion about ways of approaching jobs.

Setting an example

Working reasonable hours

If your behaviour contradicts what you say, you will send mixed messages to your colleagues. The way that you behave will have more impact than your words, and your example will carry more weight than what you say. It is no good encouraging others to adopt stress-preventive strategies unless you are seen to put them into practice yourself.

Scene 40: Joan's long hours

Kyra looks at the clock and starts to put her belongings away in her bag. 'I'll just get the bus if I leave now,' she says. She looks across at Joan, who is frowning at her computer screen in concentration.

'Fine,' says Joan abstractedly. 'I'll carry on for a bit until I get this timetable sorted.'

Kyra hesitates. 'We got quite a lot done today. Can't we finish it tomorrow?'

'I'd just like to get it done. Don't worry, you get off.'

Kyra does go home, but feels guilty. It is difficult not to feel that she should have worked late as well. Joan always encourages her team not to stay at work too long, but she herself puts in very long hours and is often the last to leave the building. In spite of what Joan says, Kyra feels under pressure to follow her example. She feels that because she doesn't constantly stay late there will be doubts about the level of her commitment to the job. After all, Joan is the team leader, and presumably her way of doing things is the right way.

ACTIVITY 49: What example do you set?

Which of the following anti-stress practices are you seen to follow? Give yourself a mark out of 10 to show how consistently your behaviour may be observed.

- Not working excessive hours
- Not praising people for working excessive hours
- Not arranging for meetings outside office hours
- Taking all your holiday entitlement
- Taking breaks during the day
- Saying no to requests
- Not accepting unrealistic deadlines
- Not sending emails to colleagues at weekends
- Saying thank you
- Giving praise

Creating a positive environment

One of the sources of stress in the workplace is feeling undervalued. Some ways in which you can affirm the value of individuals include:

- offering praise or recognition for good work;
- showing people that their opinion and their work counts;
- being interested in people as individuals.

ACTIVITY 50: Ways of tackling stress in your workplace

Choose three of the following suggestions that you could put into practice. For each one that you have chosen, identify four steps that you need to take to set it up. Commit yourself to a starting date for the process.

	1	2	3	4	Date
Working party to assess stress levels					
Stress audits					
Counselling advice lines					
Referral to treatment services					
Stress awareness training					
Time management training					
Assertion/communication course					
Management training					
Anti-bullying policy					
Anti-harassment policy					
System for airing grievances					
Appraisal programme					
Exercise classes					
Relaxation therapies					
Lifestyle management courses					
Your own ideas					

Keep your eye on the ball

As you know, people's response to pressure varies as work and individual circumstances change. Maintain your awareness of the situation at work. Make sure that systems and processes are followed through, and – most important – keep the lines of communication open.

8

Stressful Jobs

Although it could be argued that every job has its share of pressure, there are certain occupations which are most frequently associated with stress-related ailments. People whose jobs have been identified as particularly stressful include:

- IT industry workers;
- teachers;
- doctors;
- nurses;
- police officers;
- prison officers;
- social workers;

- air traffic controllers;
- armed forces;
- ambulance workers;
- government workers;
- middle managers;
- secretaries.

Why these occupations are stressful

The factors which contribute to stress in these professions are those which we have discussed in previous chapters. What makes workers in these jobs particularly vulnerable to stress could be the frequency and intensity of the pressure they experience. For example, some doctors work punishingly long hours, during which they are required to exercise judgement on crucial matters and to remain calm. Social workers and teachers report that they constantly suffer from an overload of paperwork and having to meet multiple targets, as well as addressing the individual needs of clients and students.

Of course, not everyone in these occupations suffers from stress, and there is nothing to say that people in occupations with a low stress rating, such as librarians, gardeners and museum curators, will never feel the harmful effects of pressure. Stress is personal, and can affect everyone. Furthermore, the pressures and stressful factors of individual occupations fluctuate with the changes that take place in the nature of jobs and in the society within which we work.

Public sector workers

Many public sector employees choose this type of work because of the potential satisfaction of being able to 'make a difference' to society and to improve the lives of individuals. Even if job satisfaction is comparatively high, the pressures of low pay, bureaucratic demands and a poor public image can lead to stress and dissatisfaction.

Ways of coping

Contact your professional organization for advice and information about dealing with the pressures in your particular work area.

Go to your GP if you suffer any stress-related symptoms.

Be realistic about time management and your workload.

Identify any habits of thought that lock you into stressful ways of working – remember that you do not need to be perfect, that you cannot be all things to all people. Accept that you do what you can within the limits of the available resources.

Make relaxation a high priority.

Look for balance – if you have little control over events at work, develop a sense of control and responsibility in other areas of your life.

Schedule time for activities that recharge and renew you.

Make active use of your support network.

Prepare ways of responding to criticisms of your profession.

Burnout in the caring professions – and others

Burnout is a term used to describe the kind of collapse caused by exhaustion and overwork that was first identified in occupations such as therapy and social work, but is now applied to financial and legal sectors and other branches of the corporate world. Tight deadlines, relentless pressure for higher productivity and the threat of downswing and layoffs contribute to physical ailments such as chronic fatigue and to feelings of failure and worthlessness.

Warning signs

These can include:

- permanent exhaustion;
- feeling angry all the time;

- feeling that you are a failure, no matter how hard you work;
- becoming cynical and humourless;
- feelings of isolation;
- compulsive activities – shopping, drinking, gambling, Internet use, etc.;
- any of the physical symptoms described in Chapter 1.

Your own ideas:

Ways of coping

Go to your GP.

Identify your precise stressors and your options for dealing with them.

Examine your goals and values.

Make your own definition of success.

Think of other ways of meeting your work needs – have an idea-generating session, talk it through with a friend. Perhaps you would be happier in another branch of your work area, practising a different kind of law, for example, or working in a behind-the-scenes role rather than dealing face-to-face with the public.

Look at non-work environments for ways of fulfilling your needs. If you make a significant change at work for the sake of your health and sanity, but still have the same motivating drives, think how you can satisfy them in leisure and social activities. If you have a competitive urge, you could channel it into sports or games which challenge you physically or mentally. If you like to manage and organize events or people, you could look for a leading role in an organization such as fund-raising, amateur dramatics, parents' associations.

Find a method of relaxation that suits you. Make it a priority to practise whichever method you choose.

Put balance back into your life. Schedule time for social and leisure activities.

Shift work

Some jobs and professions have to meet the demands of our 24-hour-day culture. Staff in hospitals, the police force, the media and the travel industry are just some of the people who work long and unsociable shifts. Continuous shift work and working into the early hours of the morning affect your physical and emotional well-being. It disrupts sleep patterns and affects your metabolic rate, as well as causing havoc with your personal and family life.

Ways of coping

Impose a regular structure by sleeping at the same time every day.

When you work a night shift, try to move around as much as possible. Do stretching exercises.

Create a night-time environment in the room in which you sleep by making it as dark as possible. You could put up thick curtains, or wear an eye mask. You could look at shift swapping, a system which lets staff negotiate their working times and shifts among themselves.

A final word

Test your knowledge!

For each of the following situations, decide which option is an example of how to manage a potentially stressful situation in a positive way.

1 You are in a noisy office and trying to concentrate on your work. A positive way for you to reduce your stress would be to:

   (a) skip lunch and work during the lunch hour when the office is quieter;
   (b) play loud music to drown out the noise;
   (c) wear more comfortable clothes to work and bring in little treats for yourself;
   (d) take breaks from the office.

2 A colleague cuts you dead when you say hello. A positive way to deal with the situation would be to:

(a) worry about what you have done to offend the person;
(b) forget it;
(c) make a point of speaking to the person as soon as possible so that you can assess if there is a problem;
(d) get your own back by spreading a nasty rumour about the person concerned.

3 You are concerned that the quality of your work isn't high enough, although you are told that you are doing a good job. A positive way for you to reduce your stress would be to:

(a) spend more time trying to improve the quality of your work;
(b) plan to have a drink with colleagues every day after work;
(c) spend more time focusing on the positive aspects of your work;
(d) look for another job that will give you more satisfaction.

4 You are very busy at work when a colleague asks for help with a project. You do not want to help out on this occasion. A positive way for you to reduce your stress would be to:

(a) help, but say you won't do it again;
(b) explain that you can't help and concentrate on your own work;
(c) pretend that you haven't heard the request and carry on working;
(d) tell your colleague that you will help when you have finished your own work.

5 Your manager asks you to take on some extra tasks. You already have a heavy workload. A positive way of handling the situation would be to:

(a) accept, and think of ways to offload the work on someone else;
(b) agree to take on the work because you do not want to seem uncommitted;
(c) discuss your priorities with your manager and look for a solution;

(d) say that you do not know how you will manage to get it done, but accept it anyway.

6 A technical assistant has prepared the slides for a presentation you are giving. During the presentation you find that some of the slides are in the wrong order. Do you:

(a) fluff what you were saying and feel embarrassed;
(b) find an excuse to leave the room so that you can burst into tears;
(c) say, 'I'll kill that technician';
(d) make a light-hearted comment and carry on seamlessly. You have made yourself very familiar with the material and can talk your way through it.

Answers: 1d 2c 3c 4b 5c 6d.

These answers describe effective ways of handling stressful situations. Remember, however, that every individual is different, and every situation is different depending on the particular individuals involved. The important thing is to recognize and acknowledge what is causing you stress, and to find your own way of dealing with it. Use this book to help you to find positive strategies that will work for you and help you to manage successfully your own individual challenges.

The joy of work

Work can be a place of learning and growth, and it can provide you with satisfaction, fulfilment, meaning and challenge. Learn to manage stress so that you always operate at your personal best, with a sense of involvement and direction.

Further Reading

The Essential Guide to Work/Life Balance, Department of Trade and Industry, 2002.

Stress and Employer Liability, Jill Earnshaw and Cary Cooper, CIPD, 2000.

Managing Anger at Work, Mary Hartley, Sheldon Press, 2002.

Work–Life Balance, Gordon and Ronni Lamont, Sheldon Press, 2001.

Depression at Work, Vicky Maud, Sheldon Press, 2000.

Keeping Well at Work – A TUC Guide, Philip Pearson, Kogan Page, 2001.

Index